The Emperor's New Clothes

or Five Beans for Jack

A Children's Play

David Foxton

A Samuel French Acting Edition

SAMUELFRENCH-LONDON.CO.UK
SAMUELFRENCH.COM

Copyright © 2011 by David Foxton
All Rights Reserved

THE EMPEROR'S NEW CLOTHES is fully protected under the copyright laws of the British Commonwealth, including Canada, the United States of America, and all other countries of the Copyright Union. All rights, including professional and amateur stage productions, recitation, lecturing, public reading, motion picture, radio broadcasting, television and the rights of translation into foreign languages are strictly reserved.

ISBN 978-0-573-15011-1

www.samuelfrench-london.co.uk

www.samuelfrench.com

FOR AMATEUR PRODUCTION ENQUIRIES

UNITED KINGDOM AND WORLD EXCLUDING NORTH AMERICA

plays@SamuelFrench-London.co.uk

020 7255 4302/01

Each title is subject to availability from Samuel French, depending upon country of performance.

CAUTION: Professional and amateur producers are hereby warned that *THE EMPEROR'S NEW CLOTHES* is subject to a licensing fee. Publication of this play does not imply availability for performance. Both amateurs and professionals considering a production are strongly advised to apply to the appropriate agent before starting rehearsals, advertising, or booking a theatre. A licensing fee must be paid whether the title is presented for charity or gain and whether or not admission is charged.

The professional rights in this play are controlled by Samuel French Ltd, 52 Fitzroy Street, London, W1T 5JR.

No one shall make any changes in this title for the purpose of production. No part of this book may be reproduced, stored in a retrieval system, or transmitted in any form, by any means, now known or yet to be invented, including mechanical, electronic, photocopying, recording, videotaping, or otherwise, without the prior written permission of the publisher. No one shall upload this title, or part of this title, to any social media websites.

The right of David Foxton to be identified as author of this work has been asserted by him in accordance with Section 77 of the Copyright, Designs and Patents Act 1988

CHARACTERS

Tom Bell, the Town Crier, known to all as "**Tink**"
Aloysius Sly, a rogue and confidence trickster, partner to Wily
Cressida Wilhelmina Wily, a rogue and confidence trickster, partner to Sly
Abigail Bell, Tink's long suffering daughter
Abacus, the Treasurer to the Court
Lord Chamberlain
Guard Captain
Emperor Persimmon, our Emperor
Empress Petronella, Emperor's wife
Jack, the young man of Beanstalk fame
Jack's Mother
2 Attendants
Courtiers, Guards, Fashion Models and stage hands

Scene: Various locations in the town.

SYNOPSIS OF SCENES

ACT I

A Town Square or Street

ACT II

Scene 1	A Street
Scene 2	The Palace

ACT III

Scene 1	A Street
Scene 2	The Palace Again!
Scene 3	Town Square Bedecked With Flags

Other plays by David Foxton published by Samuel French Ltd:

Breakfast For One
Card Play
Oubliette
Perkin and the Pastrycook
Rabbit
The Real Story of Puss in Boots

ACT I

A Town Square or Street

No one is about. A Town Crier enters. He is obviously disorganized for he keeps dropping his papers, even his bells as he walks on. His name is Tom Bell, nicknamed Tink, which is short for Tinker. He decides on where he will stand then moves a little. He gets himself ready to speak — a few preliminary coughs then he begins

Tink (*ringing his bell*) Oyez! (*Ringing*) Oyez! (*Ringing*) Oyez! (*Breaking out of his Town Crier mode to speak to the audience*) This is a most important job you know — most important. I proclaim the news and... and... things. I'm the Crier, not a boo-hoo crier, a sort of yoo-hoo crier for the town. Me. I'll start again. (*Ringing*) Oyez! (*Ringing*) Oyez! That'll do... just two... Ladies and gentlepersons, townsfolk and bystanders, visitors, and all my friends and relatives especially all those who live down our street and all you people sitting at the back, and all of you down here at the front — not forgetting those of you in the middle of course. (*Ringing*) I have a most important proclamation... (*More throat clearing as he sorts out his papers — badly; ringing*) Now hear this... (*Reading*) "One small brown loaf, half a dozen medium sized eggs, a pound of cheddar cheese — mature, four large onions, half a pound of two-penny rice..." (*Realizing this is not correct*) Wait a minute. No. That's not it. That's the wrong proclamation. That's the shopping list. Now where's the — ah here we are. This must be it. (*Ringing*) It's me back again. (*Ringing*) Are you still receiving me? Now hear this... (*Reading*) "Dear all, we are having a nice time here at the seaside. The weather is fine and we have been swimming every day. Little Paul ate a bucket of sand yesterday and was sick all over Auntie Doris's carpet. Tomorrow..." (*Realizing this also is incorrect*) No, that can't be it either. That's a letter from Uncle Dan and Auntie Bronwen. Just give me a moment. I know I've got a proclamation somewhere. I thought I had it in this pocket. I could have sworn that I did... Let me see... (*He sorts through his papers*)

As he does so, Sly and Wily — two somewhat shifty characters, tricksters — enter and approach him

Sly Don't tell me, don't tell me. You must undoubtedly be the Town Crier of this most attractive place. Am I right?
Tink What?
Sly You are the Town Crier, are you not?
Tink I am indeed, sir. I am.
Sly And it's pleased to meet you that we are. Could I take the liberty of introducing myself? The name is Sly, Aloysius Sly. And my companion here is ——
Wily Cressida Wilhelmina Wily. Call me Wily — for short.
Tink Tom Bell, "Tink"' to almost everyone.
Sly Well, how amazingly fortunate, Mr Tink, that having just arrived in your truly...
Wily Ordinary...
Sly (*nudging Wily for saying the "wrong" word*) Appealing little town. We should meet up with the very man who can help us.
Wily Assist us.
Sly Guide us.
Wily Inform us.
Sly Tell us.
Tink Why? Is there something you want to know?
Sly I knew it, Wily. We have, by mere chance, met up with a fellow who catches on readily.
Wily What perspicacity.
Sly Such a quick brain.
Tink Can I help you in some way?
Sly Indeed you can.
Wily We need to find our way to the Palace.
Sly Of the Emperor... er... the Emperor...?
Wily The Emperor...?
Tink Emperor Persimmon?
Sly That's him.
Wily Your Emperor.
Tink Oh, he's not just mine. The Emperor for the whole country you know.
Sly Really?
Wily And he has a wife?
Tink Of course he has. Petronella...
Sly Write it all down, Wily.
Wily I'm doing just that.
Sly So where will we find this illustrious monarch?
Tink Who?
Sly The Emperor... and his court?

Act I 3

Tink At the palace — straight on down here, then first right and the palace is up the hill to the left. You can't miss it.
Wily You've been so helpful. Thank you.
Sly Yes. Many thanks. In fact... Wait. Help of this kind deserves — a reward. Here Mr Tink, (*giving him a banknote*) have twenty pounds — for your pains.
Tink Pains? But I don't have any. Perhaps the odd twinge in my knees after a long day.
Sly You've been most helpful.
Wily (*to Sly*) The man's a buffoon.
Sly (*to Wily*) Come on. We need to find the palace. And see what's what. Thanks again, Mr Tink.

They exit SR

Tink You're welcome. What nice people. And twenty pounds to spend. Now if I could just find that proclamation I'd be... laughing. Well, smiling anyway. Where on earth did I put it?

Tink's daughter, Abigail, enters SL

Abigail Have you finished, Father? It's high time you came home, Mother says. She says you should have done all your proclaiming by now.
Tink Abi, I haven't finished. I haven't even started. I can't find the proclamation. I've lost it.
Abigail Mother says if you don't come home right away, there'll be no dinner for you.
Tink No dinner! Oh yes, there will be dinner for me, and you and her. Because I've just earned twenty pounds. Look. (*He shows her the banknote*)

Abigail takes it

And there's a lesson to be learned there, my child. If you help people in need, if you give them some of your time, you will be rewarded.
Abigail (*giving the banknote back*) It's a forgery.
Tink What?
Abigail It's a fake. It's not real.
Tink Not real — of course it's real. What makes you think it isn't?
Abigail Well, if you look closely you'll see that the twenty is not quite printed straight and the Emperor's face is too dark, and the signature is a bit smudged and anyway along the top there it says "Bank of Toyland".

Tink Toyland?
Abigail You've been tricked, father. It's play money, it's not real.
Tink Toyland?
Abigail Now are you coming home or not?
Tink (*to audience*) I've been fooled... by those two. That's not nice, is it?
Abigail Come on. Forget it. Dinnertime.
Tink No! I must find the proclamation, I must tell it to the town.
Abigail How can you if you don't know where it is?
Tink I must have dropped it. And it's blown away. Let's just have a look round.
Abigail (*to audience*) Excuse me, I'm sorry to interrupt but I wonder if you would be so kind as to help my father — the Town Crier — he was going to make this announcement and he seems to have mislaid it. Perhaps one of you might have seen it or found it even. Perhaps you wouldn't mind just looking around under your seats possibly. It's a piece of paper with writing on it.

Abigail and Tink leave the stage for the auditorium — leaving the bell onstage — to look for the missing proclamation, talking to the audience as they do so. Tink may well say "I've just been tricked you know", etc

Come on, Father. You look over there, I'll look over here.

Should any member of the audience proffer a piece of paper — perhaps a programme or a ticket whatever — Tink should try it out as the proclamation before saying "No... no... That can't be it"

Indeed it would be a good idea to use a programme in this way. If a paper is offered to Abigail she refers it to Tink — "Is this it?", "What about this?", etc.

As Tink and Abigail are looking, the Lord Chamberlain enters SL *escorted by Abacus, the Treasurer, and the Guard Captain. He looks around pompously, sees what is going on, picks up the bell and rings it*

Tink and Abigail freeze with a sharp intake of breath

Abigail Did you do that?
Tink No. Did you do that?
Abigail No.
Lord Chamberlain I did it. It was me! I want a word with you, Crier, about a certain proclamation.

Act I

Tink and Abigail return to the stage

Tink (*as he returns*) Oh, no! Oh, heck! Oh, dear! Forgive me, your Lordship. Mercy, I beg you. I don't know how it happened. I didn't mean it. I don't know what to say... except that I apologize, I'm sorry. I'll just have to take my punishment like a —— (*He falls on his knees to the Lord Chamberlain*)
Lord Chamberlain Stop mumbling and whining, fellow, and do get off your knees. You make me feel like an archbishop, and I'm much more important than that.
Tink (*rising*) You are indeed, Lord Chamberlain.
Lord Chamberlain About the proclamation...
Tink Oh, dear.
Abigail My father didn't mean it, my Lord.
Lord Chamberlain Do be quiet child! About the proclamation. (*To Abacus*) Do we have it?
Tink No.
Abacus Yes, my Lord — here it is. (*He hands the proclamation to the Lord Chamberlain*)
Lord Chamberlain Thank you, Abacus.
Tink I thought I had it.
Abigail (*exasperated*) Oh, Father!
Lord Chamberlain You do *now*. (*Handing it over*) It's about the Emperor's birthday celebrations.
Abigail Has that come round again?
Lord Chamberlain Indeed it has. It's time for presents and processions... Oh, and there's also a bit about the forged banknotes.
Tink Forgeries?
Abacus Forged banknotes. We've noticed, at the treasury, a number of forged banknotes. They are being spread about by tricksters of some kind. We need to stop them. So anyone found with a forged banknote of any value will be immediately imprisoned and their possessions seized by the Guard Captain.
Tink Imprisoned? Seized?
Lord Chamberlain That doesn't worry you, does it, Crier?
Tink Of course not. (*Trembling and passing the banknote to Abigail*) Why should it?
Lord Chamberlain So read us the proclamation.
Tink What? Now?
Lord Chamberlain I always like to hear how the words sound. I write a good proclamation though I say it myself. I have a way with words. Read it!

Somewhat agitatedly and certainly with more than a modicum of apprehension, Tink rings and shouts weedily

Tink (*ringing*) Oyez! (*Ringing*) Oyez!
Lord Chamberlain Oh, give it more than that. You're a Town Crier not a town whisperer.
Tink (*bigger; ringing*) Oyez! (*Coughing nervously; softly*) By order of His Lordship, the Grand...
Lord Chamberlain Louder! Louder, fellow!
Tink (*loudly*) By order of His Lordship, the Grand Chamberpot...
Lord Chamberlain What? Lord Chamber*lain* — *lain* not *pot*.
Tink Sorry, Chamber—lain. It is decreed that the official birthday of his knobbly Majesty ——
Lord Chamberlain —noble Majesty.
Tink — noble Majesty, Emperor Persimmon the twerp...
Lord Chamberlain The twelfth, the twelfth. The Emperor is not a twerp, is he Abacus?
Abacus Er... Could I have further notice of that question?
Tink It's just that I'm so nervous, my Lord. I want to get it right — Persimmon the Twelfth, will be concentrated——
Lord Chamberlain —celebrated.
Tink — next Friday. There will be ——
Lord Chamberlain —a procession, in which I shall feature large, and impressively and it will be led by the Emperor in the most sumptuous of garments, and bejewelled, riding his best white stallion, and accompanied by the Empress——
Tink — Umberella——
Lord Chamberlain —Petronella, together with their entire entourage. The day will of course be a public holiday and the Emperor will receive presents from his loyal subjects at the Palace between half past ten and twelve noon.
Tink Long live the Emperor!
Lord Chamberlain Indeed! Now the P.S.
Tink The P.S.?

The Lord Chamberlain points at it on the scroll

Oh, yes. (*Ringing a smaller bell taken from his pocket*) P.S. Any person or persons found in possession of forged banknotes will be subject to instant imprisonment and the forfeiture of their property. (*He groans*)
Abacus By order of Treasurer Abacus — that's me!
Lord Chamberlain So off you go, Crier, spread the word to all parts of the Town. Meantime I will ensure that the same information is sent

Act I 7

to all parts of the country. We need the royal birthday to be a grand celebration.
Abacus It will be an expensive one. The country can't afford too many celebrations.
Lord Chamberlain We can always tax the people more — to pay for these events.
Abacus We taxed them last time.
Lord Chamberlain So we know it works. Go on, Crier, don't wait around — get on with the proclaiming.
Tink I'm going, I'm going. (*To Abigail*) Tell your mother I'll be late home, Abigail.

He exits through the audience

Abigail Bye.
Lord Chamberlain And we'll get back to the palace. There must be some lists to make.
Abacus And bills to pay.
Guard Captain And prisoners to lock up for having forged banknotes.
Lord Chamberlain So much to do, so little time. Let's go.

Abacus and the Guard Captain make to go

No! Wait! It's me first. Who's Grand Lord Chamberlain?
Abacus
Guard Captain } (*together*) You are, my Lord.
Lord Chamberlain So I go first and you follow. Come along.

The three exit SL

Abigail Oh dear, I hope my father does it right. He's not really a good Town Crier. He makes too many mistakes, especially when he's nervous. And what can I do about this forged banknote? If I'm caught with it, I could end up in prison. I could throw it away or hide it? (*She looks round to see if there is somewhere to hide it*)

Sly and Wily enter SR

Wily I said he was a buffoon. We shouldn't have taken his directions.
Sly But he's the Town Crier.
Wily I don't care if he's Lord Mayor, he's a fool and he sent us the wrong way.
Sly So where do you reckon the Palace is then?

Wily How should I know?

They see Abigail who is still musing about what she might do with the forged banknote. Sly indicates he will speak to her but Wily indicates "No" — she will do it

Wily Good day, my dear, and what are you doing?
Abigail (*hiding the note*) Doing? Nothing. I'm doing nothing — nothing at all. Absolutely nothing.
Wily Well, in that case perhaps you would be prepared to help us. You see me and my friend here——
Sly — are lost.
Abigail Lost?
Wily Well, not completely lost — we just need a little help.
Sly With some directions.
Wily To the palace.
Abigail The Royal palace?
Wily How many palaces do you have?
Sly The one where your Emperor resides.
Abigail Oh, the Emperor's Royal Palace.
Wily That's the one.
Sly The stupid idiot who calls himself the Town Crier sent us in the wrong direction completely.
Wily The man's a nincompoop.
Abigail That's my father.

Sly and Wily are taken aback

Sly }
Wily } (*together*) Ah! Is it?
Sly It must have been a slip of the tongue.
Wily An easily made mistake.
Sly Not intentional.
Wily No. He must have been preoccupied.
Sly Thinking of other — bigger things.
Wily Pressured.
Sly Stress.
Abigail Well, it's kind of you to be so understanding, he has been a bit forgetful recently.
Sly Forgetful?
Abigail Yes. He thought he'd lost a most important proclamation and then found out that the Grand Lord Chamberlain hadn't actually given him it.

Act I 9

Wily An important proclamation?
Sly About what? What's so important?
Abigail It was about the Emperor's Birthday Celebrations.
Sly Birthday Celebrations?
Wily Those could be expensive.
Sly Those could cost a lot.
Wily The Emperor might need advisers. (*He indicates the two of them*)
Abigail He might well.
Sly And that's what we're here for. So tell us. Which way is the palace — the Emperor's palace?
Abigail (*pointing off left*) That way, first left, second right — you can't miss it.
Wily I've heard that before.
Sly So kind.
Wily So very kind.
Sly Have a reward. (*He hands her a banknote*)
Wily You deserve it my dear.

They scamper off SL

Abigail Thank you — have a nice day. (*Looking at the "reward"*) Oh! Five pounds, that's nice. That's kind. That's... Wait a minute. "Bank of Toyland". It's another forgery. They passed me a forged banknote. What am I going to do if I get caught? Oh, heavens. (*She sits, woebegone and sad*)

Jack enters SR, *and approaches Abigail. He has a length of rope which trails offstage behind him. (It is he of later Beanstalk fame)*

Jack Abi... Are you all right?
Abigail (*hiding the money behind her*) I haven't got any — honestly.
Jack What are you talking about?
Abigail Oh, it's you, Jack. I was thinking of something else entirely. Where are you going?
Jack I'm glad you asked that, Abi, cos I'm doing a job that needs to be done. Mother has decided we must sell the cow.
Abigail What, Milky White — your only cow?
Jack Yep! We need the money, Mother says. So I'm going to sell her. (*He shows the rope*)
Abigail Won't you miss her?
Jack She'll be at home when I get back.
Abigail Not your mother — Milky White, the cow.
Jack Oh, yes! I will miss her. Come on, Milky.

He moves across the stage and exits SL. *The rope follows — there's nothing on the end of it!*

Abigail (*picking up the end of the rope*) Jack! Jack!

Jack returns

Jack Milky White, how you've changed!
Abigail It's me, Jack — you've forgotten the cow.
Jack (*taking the rope from her*) Thanks, Abi. I'll have to go back and get her.

He exits SR

Abigail shakes her head despairingly. She sits disconsolate

A fanfare

The Guard Captain enters SL

Guard Captain Make way for the entourage of his Highness, the Emperor Persimmon the Twelfth...

The Emperor and Empress enter together with the Lord Chamberlain and Abacus. Abacus carries a ledger

Emperor And flags! Lots and lots of flags! Bunting all across the streets. Write it down, Chamberlain. Write it down while it's fresh in my mind.
Lord Chamberlain But of course, Sire. Write it down, Abacus.
Abacus Me?
Lord Chamberlain Do it!
Emperor So, we do a left turn at the green and come straight on down here. The streets all lined with peasants cheering and waving.
Empress I didn't notice them, Persimmon.
Emperor No — they weren't there today but they will be there for the procession, the real procession. Will they have things to wave, Chamberlain?
Lord Chamberlain Will they have things to wave, Abacus?
Abacus Their hands, your Majesty?
Emperor No. They need something else to wave — something brighter and better and cleaner than hands.
Abacus (*writing down*) No hands.

Act I   11

Emperor More flags! That's it! More flags! The peasants will have flags — see to it, Chamberlain.
Lord Chamberlain How many, your Majesty?
Emperor All of them!
Lord Chamberlain No, Sire. How many flags?
Emperor One each.
Lord Chamberlain One each hand?
Emperor No — one each peasant. That should be enough, don't you think my dear?
Empress It will be splendid I'm sure, Persimmon, and I will be radiant and magnificent.
Emperor Of course you will, my love, that goes without saying. And the bands will play. We must have several bands and bagpipes.
Lord Chamberlain Bagpipes!
Emperor Such stirring music. I'll be in front of course and then the Palace Guard Captain and the Cavalry and banners. We must have banners. Write it all down, Chamberlain. I feel inspired.
Lord Chamberlain Banners, Abacus.
Abacus I heard.
Emperor Fluttering in the breeze. We must have a slight breeze. See to it.
Abacus (*how?*) Breeze?
Emperor And when we reach here, surrounded by all my loyal subjects. All cheering and waving their flags.
Abacus In the breeze.
Emperor Yes! Yes! The Parade will halt and I will dismount. Help me down, Guard Captain.
Guard Captain But you aren't up, Sire!
Emperor But I will be. I will be. Help me down. Pretend to help me down.

The Guard Captain does so

> And I shall do a sort of walkabout, greeting the people. (*He moves about the stage waving to the imaginary crowd. Ad-libbing: "Hallo subjects", "So pleased to see you", etc.*)

The Guard Captain goes to the Empress and makes to "help her down"

Empress What on earth are you doing, Guard Captain?
Guard Captain Helping *you* down too, your Majesty.
Empress I'm not up. I'm in a carriage.
Lord Chamberlain Carriage, Abacus.

Abacus (*noting it*) One royal carriage.
Empress And six horses.
Abacus Six! Six? Do we need six, your Majesty?
Empress If he's having a breeze, I want six horses.
Lord Chamberlain Just write it all down, Abacus.
Emperor Perhaps, I've just thought. Perhaps I should actually speak to a peasant or two. You know like — have a conversation.
Empress With a peasant?
Emperor A loyal, flag-waving peasant. What d'you think, Chamberlain?
Lord Chamberlain Brilliant, Sire. A stroke of genius.
Empress But what would you say?
Emperor Er... "Hallo peasant" and the peasant would reply — er... What? What would the reply be, Chamberlain?

The Lord Chamberlain shrugs

Emperor Abacus?

A similar shrug from Abacus

I know... Guard Captain, you are a peasant.
Guard Captain No, Sire. I'm a Guard Captain — your Guard Captain — at the palace. You remember?
Emperor Yes, I know but just pretend that you're a peasant.
Guard Captain Right, Sire. What do I do?
Emperor Wave.

The Guard Captain waves his hand

No. Your flag, wave your flag.
Guard Captain I haven't got one, Sire.
Emperor Pretend, man. Pretend. And I say, "Hallo, peasant" and what do you say?
Guard Captain I give up, Sire. What do I say?
Emperor Why isn't anything going right? We were all right till the procession stopped, and I started to be pleasant with a peasant.
Guard Captain Can I stop being a peasant now, Sire?
Emperor Did you ever start? Oh, how can I plan the procession properly? How can I make sure the celebrations will go to plan when I have to do all the thinking, all the detailed arrangements myself? I mean — if I talk to a peasant, what will it reply?

No one on stage knows, but Abigail offers an answer

Act I

Abigail Happy Birthday, your Majesty!
Emperor Who said that?
Abigail I did, your Highness.
Emperor Look! Look! A genuine peasant. My dear, look what it is. A peasant. And it spoke, it replied. Did you write that down, Chamberlain?
Lord Chamberlain (*to Abacus*) Did we?

Abacus nods

We did!
Emperor (*to the Empress*) My dear... See? A peasant and it spoke.
Empress I heard it.
Emperor Have you got a name, peasant?
Abigail Abi, your Majesty. Abi Bell, the Town Crier's daughter.
Emperor Yes, yes — right! Well, that's enough conversation, peasant! So then I turn away from the crowds and join the procession again and we go... Where do we go next, Chamberlain?
Lord Chamberlain To the cathedral, for the service of thanksgiving for your reign, and your health, and your future happiness, and... all that sort of thing.
Emperor Yes! Yes! I can see it already. Oh, yes. The cathedral and inside there'll be flags.
Abacus More flags?
Emperor So let's go. Come on, this way.
Guard Captain No! No! Your Highness.
Emperor What d'you mean "No", Guard Captain? I'm Emperor and I say "Yes".
Guard Captain But you haven't got back up.
Emperor Up?
Guard Captain On the horse. The horse.
Emperor Horse? (*He looks round bewilderedly*)
Empress Oh, get in the carriage with me, Persimmon. It will save time.
Emperor Good thinking, my dear. And the whole parade will move off to the cathedral and the crowd will wave and cheer.
Abigail (*clapping on her own*) Hooray!

She might encourage the audience to join in

Emperor Isn't it wonderful to be popular? Thank you! Thank you! Marvellous. Wait. Where's the band?

Lord Chamberlain It's behind us, your Majesty. Playing as we parade down to the cathedral.
Emperor Of course. Do it, Chamberlain. Be the band so I get the feel of it.
Lord Chamberlain Me? Be a band?
Emperor The three of you. (*To Abigail*) You too, peasant. Play something stirring. Ready, off we go. Play!

They move off and exit SR, *the Lord Chamberlain, Abacus, the Guard Captain and Abigail being the band playing "The Entry of the Gladiators"!*

Sly and Wily run on SL

Wily These military bands get worse and worse.
Sly Never mind about the music. We must catch up with the Emperor. We need to make ourselves known to him. We need to make him *need* us.
Wily They ought to have more trombones, more brass generally.
Sly Shut up about the band. You've delayed us enough already.
Wily But we couldn't miss a chance like that.
Sly Trust you to want to buy a cow.
Wily It's called Milky White.
Sly It doesn't matter what it's called. We don't need a cow.
Wily It was a bargain — a snip.
Sly How much did you pay?
Wily This is the best bit. I paid him five beans. That's all.
Sly Five beans?
Wily A bean, a bean and a half, two beans and half a bean — five.
Sly He sold you his cow for just five beans?
Wily Yes — but I told him they were magic beans and he believed me.
Sly You sly rascal.
Wily No — *you're* Sly. I'm Wily.

There is a mooing sound, off R

And the cow's on the green.
Sly All's right with the world. So let's get on after the Emperor. Which way do you think he went?
Wily Follow the band.
Sly (*listening*) It's very faint, very faint indeed. Come on. It's somewhere in this direction.

Act I   15

They exit SR

We hear a mooing sound off R *then Tink's bell ringing*

Tink enters via the auditorium

Tink (*ringing his bell*) Oyez! Oyez! Oyez! Phew! This is hard work. I've been right down as far as the river proclaiming. (*Reaching the stage; ringing*) Oyez! (*Ringing*) Oyez! (*Ringing*) Oyez! By order of His Lordship the Grand Chamber... lain. It is decreed that the official birthday of his... noble... Majesty Emperor Persimmon the Twerp... Oops! Twelfth... will be celebrated every Friday... Wait a minute! I've been here before. I've proclaimed here earlier. I'd better move on. (*To the audience*) No disrespect. I'll go down towards the green. (*Indicating left*) This way.

Tink exits SL, *ringing his bell*

Abigail enters SR

Abigail Father! Father! Missed him. Oh, heavens! What am I going to do about this forged money? It must be those two who gave me this note who are passing them round. What shall I do? I wonder.

Jack meanders in SL

Jack I've just heard your Dad, Abi. Down near the green. He was proclaiming to Milky White.
Abigail Jack! Have you left your cow down there then?
Jack Nope.
Abigail So what's she doing on the green?
Jack Eating and mooing and listening to your Dad's proclamation. And anyway, she's not my cow any more.
Abigail You've sold her? You've sold Milky White?
Jack I've done just that. Mother will be so pleased. These two folk really took a fancy to the cow, so I was able to sell her really easily.
Abigail Two people? Jack, they... didn't ... pay... you...
Jack Course they did. That's what selling's all about, Abi.
Abigail No. I meant — in notes — banknotes.
Jack No. They didn't give me banknotes, paper money.
Abigail Oh, thank heavens.
Jack No. They gave me five beans.
Abigail Beans!?

Jack Five of them — not bad, eh, Abi?
Abigail You sold your cow Milky White for five beans.
Jack No.
Abigail I thought you just said you did.
Jack I was wrong.
Abigail Thank goodness.
Jack It was five *magic* beans.
Abigail Magic? Magic beans. Oh, Jack, what have you done? They've tricked you. They took advantage of you. They've made a fool out of you.
Jack Won't my mother be pleased?
Abigail How could you, Jack?
Jack Five magic beans. I'd better get off home and give mother the good news. Bye, Abi!

He exits via the auditorium

Abigail (*bewildered*) Bye, Jack!

From offstage L there is loud mooing and bell ringing and a few "Oyezs". From offstage R there is the sound of the band returning — perhaps "playing" a different tune

The Emperor and his "entourage" enter. The "band" is playing very badly. They are out of breath

Emperor And we're back here... with the crowds still waving joyously, pleased to see their Emperor once again...
Empress And his beautiful wife, the Empress...
Emperor Of course, of course... and the parade can halt again... Perhaps the band might play a few gentle waltz tunes...
Lord Chamberlain Or they could have a rest...
Abacus To regain their breath...
Guard Captain Yeah...
Emperor Possibly... possibly... and shall I dismount from my noble white charger?
Empress We're in a carriage, Persimmon.
Abacus Drawn by four horses.
Empress Six! I specifically said "six".
Emperor So we get out... and speak to the crowd again... (*Nudging Abigail*) Hallo, peasant!
Abigail Not now, your Majesty, I've got things on my mind.

Act I   17

Emperor On your mind! Good grief! You're a peasant, you're not supposed to have a mind.

Sly and Wily enter, masked and cloaked, with weapons

Sly Stand where you are!
Wily Go no further!
Sly Two villainous rogues.
Wily And thieving vagabonds jump out of the crowd and take the Emperor and his wife prisoner.

Sly and Wily do just this

Sly Your Majesties — you are our prisoners.
Wily The band can do nothing to help.
Guard Captain But the Captain of the Guard leaps to save them.
Sly No, he doesn't — you're the band.
Wily So the Emperor and Empress are captured.
Sly
Wily } (*together*) Ta- ra!
Emperor I don't remember planning this as part of our procession.
Empress What is going off, Persimmon? What does it all mean — who are these dreadful people?
Emperor Chamberlain?
Lord Chamberlain We're writing it all down as fast as we can, your Highness.
Abacus What came after "The band can do nothing to help"?
Empress Who are they?
Guard Captain They said they were rogues and something elses.
Abigail Vagabonds.
Sly Quiet, peasant!
Emperor And are we your prisoners?
Sly No, Sire!
Wily It's not true.
Sly Not at all true.
Emperor I could have sworn you said we were.
Sly It's pretend — make-believe.
Wily We pretended to attack your procession and to take you prisoners.
Empress What on earth for ?
Sly Your Majesties, bear with us. We *pretended* to attack you.
Wily We *pretended* to capture you.
Sly So that you would realize how easily it can be done.
Wily To show you need protection.

Sly Security.
Guard Captain But that's me.
Wily Bandsmen don't protect anything.
Sly After all, you don't really want your parade attacked, your birthday procession spoiled... your lives threatened, do you?
Emperor Certainly not.
Empress Most certainly not.
Emperor You know, we are most grateful to you for making this clear to us. Security is most important. (*To the Guard Captain*) Why didn't we realize it, Guard Captain? You should have been more alert instead of playing your trombone.
Guard Captain Euphonium.
Emperor I really do need some person with experience of these matters — real experience.
Sly And expertise.
Wily And skill.
Emperor To advise me on such issues of national security on royal occasions.
Sly Persons you can really really trust.
Emperor Where can I find such advisers?
Sly Where indeed?
Wily A rare commodity.

Pause

Emperor Wait a moment. I've just had an amazing thought. Couldn't you two be my special advisers?
Sly What an astounding idea.
Wily The two of us? Could we do it?
Sly Have we got the time?
Lord Chamberlain ⎫
Abacus ⎬ (*together*) No!
Guard Captain ⎭
Sly ⎫
Wily ⎬ (*together*) With pleasure, your Majesty.
Sly We would be pleased to be your special advisers.
Emperor Excellent! Chamberlain, just sign these two good people on as my Personal Advisers.
Lord Chamberlain But I advise you, Sire.
Emperor Personal Advisers whom I trust implicitly. (*To Sly and Wily*) You've met my wife, the Empress?
Sly (*kissing her hand*) Absolutely charmed — such a gracious person.
Empress What a nice man.

Act I

Wily We're proud to serve you, your Majesties.
Emperor And this is my Chamberlain... and Abacus who looks after all my money.
Sly Money?
Wily All the money?
Sly
Wily } (*together*) So very pleased to meet *you*.
Sly My name is Horatio Trust.
Wily And I am Lady Honoria Promise.
Sly You can rely on us absolutely.
Emperor (*gesturing to Abigail*) And this is a peasant.
Sly She can't help it.
Wily Pitiful creature.
Abigail Your Highness, are you sure you're doing the right thing?

An intake of breath from all the others

Empress What?
Emperor What?
Abigail You wouldn't want to be... tricked.
Emperor (*pause*) Ha! Ha! What a joke! Ha! Ha! Stupid peasant — be off with you. Guard Captain, just help her on her way.
Guard Captain (*grabbing Abigail*) Come on you!

Abigail struggles and ad libs cries to release her

Tink approaches — ringing his bell — and enters,

Tink (*ringing*) Oyez! (*Ringing*) Oyez! (*Ringing*) Oyez! Now hear this! By order of His Lordship the Great Chamber... lain. It is decreed that the official birthday... (*Looking around*) Sorry! I've been here before. I must make a note of where I proclaim. Perhaps I should have a map of some kind. Sorry! Sorry to interrupt. (*To Abigail*) Hallo Abi... Who's your friend? (*Ringing*) Don't mind me. I'll go down towards the cathedral. (*He makes to go right*)
Emperor No... Wait! I haven't heard the proclamation. Come back here you Crier fellow and let me hear it.
Lord Chamberlain It's beautifully written, your Highness.
Abacus Every word is a gem.
Lord Chamberlain How do *you* know?
Abacus You told me so.
Tink What? You want me to proclaim. Here? Now?
Emperor For me! I want to hear it.

Tink (*to the Emperor*) I'm the Town Crier you know.
Emperor And I'm the Emperor you know.

Tink begins to shake. He is nervous

So proclaim. Don't be nervous.
Tink Er... er... er...
Lord Chamberlain Ring the bell, Tinker. The bell.
Emperor Tinkerbell — such a quaint name.
Tink (*ringing*) Oyez! (*Ringing*) Oyez! (*Ringing*) Oyez! (*Gaining some control*) By order of His Lordship the Great Chamber... lain. It is decreed that the official birthday of his... noble... Majesty, Emperor Persimmon the Twelfth, will be celebrated every Friday between half past ten and twelve noon and it will be a public holiday. Long Live the Emperor.

The Emperor applauds wildly. The rest are stunned

Lord Chamberlain What else did you proclaim?
Tink (*ringing small bell*) P.S. And anybody who has a forged banknote will be locked up.
Abacus (*to Lord Chamberlain*) Did *you* write that?
Empress Persimmon, was this your idea?
Emperor I liked it. Well done, Crier.
Empress A celebration of your official birthday?
Emperor Yes! Yes!
Empress *Every* Friday!!! Who wrote this drivel? Was it you, Lord Chamberlain?
Lord Chamberlain I never wrote "Every Friday". The Crier got it wrong.
Abacus The country could never afford it.
Lord Chamberlain I'd never write anything like that.
Abacus Once a year is expensive enough but an official birthday every week.
Sly Sounds like a good idea to me.
Wily And to me... and one that befits a monarch of such stature and importance.
Emperor Did he say *every* week?
Lord Chamberlain He did indeed.
Tink I must have learnt it wrongly.
Abacus And you've told the whole town?
Tink I thought it must be a new idea.
Sly New? It's brilliant — you are a genius, Sire!

Act I   21

Emperor Am I?
Wily Birthday celebrations every week.
Sly A procession every week.
Wily Bands... Flags...
Sly Fireworks...
Wily Presents...
Emperor I like it! I like it! Oh yes, I can see it all. A party every Friday and each week a new parade, new flags, marching bands, majorettes...
Sly Elephants.
Abacus Elephants?
Wily The sky's the limit.
Sly And each time, Sire, you and the Empress will look splendid, magnificent, clad in the finest. Rich, bejewelled.
Emperor I can see it, I can see it.
Abacus Where will the money come from for all this?
Emperor The world will hear of it.
Sly The world will know you. Envy you.
Emperor Yes! Yes! Oh, most definitely yes! I can't wait. A super birthday every week — with a cake and candles. Presents galore... A different procession each time. Spectacular fireworks! New things... Everything new each time. How regal. How wonderful.
Abacus How expensive. (*He looks in his ledger*)

The Lord Chamberlain and the Guard Captain join him

Empress And jewels for me — new diamonds, new rubies.
Emperor Fur, cloaks and trimmings.
Empress Tiaras, necklaces, bracelets, earrings.

Sly and Wily are with the Emperor and Empress

Abigail Look what you've done, Father.
Tink What?

Abigail explains to her father (silently)

Emperor New horses.
Sly From Vienna.
Lord Chamberlain Vienna?
Wily Lots of ermine and silks.
Sly Satins, velvets.
Emperor I can just picture me.

Empress Us! Picture us.

They do

Abacus It'll ruin the country.
Lord Chamberlain That idiotic Town Crier!
Abacus It'll cost an arm and a leg — every week!
Lord Chamberlain And remember, we'll be expected to change for each parade.
Guard Captain I've only got one uniform. Will I need one a week?
Abacus Oh, no!
Lord Chamberlain How much do we have?
Abacus See for yourselves.

The Lord Chamberlain and the Guard Captain look at the ledger

Abigail (*to Tink*) You got it wrong.
Tink I tried to learn it, Abi.
Abigail Well, you didn't learn it correctly.
Tink Fancy a public holiday *every* Friday!
Abigail Thanks to you. And what are we going to do about these forged notes? (*She shows them to Tink*)
Tink I don't know, Abi.
Abigail Wait a bit. You got one from two strangers. And so did I?
Tink Yes.
Abigail And look at those two talking to the Emperor. Could it be ——?
Tink I'm not sure.

Abigail walks boldly over to Sly and Wily

Abigail Excuse me but I think these belong to you.
Sly What?
Wily Us?
Sly No! No! They're forgeries. Guard Captain there's someone here with forged money.
Guard Captain Where?
Sly This peasant!
Empress Seize her! Imprison her!
Emperor Do it now!
Guard Captain Right!

Abigail avoids him and runs down SR *aisle*

Act I

Emperor Catch her!

Ad-lib chase down the aisle, Abigail pursued by the Guard Captain and out through the auditorium door

As Abigail comes out, Jack runs in via the other door and aisle pursued by his mother with a besom

Jack (*as he enters*) I'm sorry! I'm sorry!
Mother Beans! I'll give you beans when I catch you. I'll separate you from your breath. Stand still so I can hit you.
Jack But they are magic beans, mother. Magic...
Mother You'll need magic to save you when I get hold of you.

They circuit the auditorium and stage and run out down the aisle they didn't use

Abigail enters, followed by the Guard Captain

Guard Captain Stop her! Catch her! Help me!

Sly and Wily advance on Abigail from the stage, slowly. The Guard Captain closes on her from the other direction. She crosses a row of the audience up and onto the stage and is helped off right by Tink. Guard Captain, Sly and Wily argue amongst themselves about whose fault it is and the three return to the stage. Meanwhile the Lord Chamberlain and Abacus have been talking money and ledgers

Emperor You let her escape.
Empress You let a peasant give you the slip.
Sly She's a slippery customer. Criminals usually are.
Wily Experienced ones are.

Jack's mother enters via her original aisle entrance. She carries a broom

Mother I'll skin him alive. He's a good-for-nothing layabout. Just wait till I get my hands on him — I'll give him such a thrashing he won't sit down for a fortnight. Jack! Where are you? (*To the audience*) You're not hiding him are you? (*To those onstage*) Have you seen him — my Jack? Well, have you?
Lord Chamberlain My good woman.

Mother (*walloping the Lord Chamberlain*) I'm no such thing! Be off with you.
Abacus Just a moment.
Mother (*walloping Abacus*) And you can go too. (*To Sly and Wily*) And what are you waiting for?

The Lord Chamberlain and Abacus leave hastily, as do Sly and Wily

Guard Captain Now see here...
Mother No, you see here... (*She wallops him*)
Emperor Do you know who I am?
Mother I don't care if you're the Emperor himself, you're wasting my time. (*She wallops him and the Empress*)

Emperor and Empress retreat, exiting left

(*To the Guard Captain*) Do you want another taste?

The Guard Captain scuttles off

(*Alone now on stage; to the audience*) When I get hold of our Jack, I shall give him a hiding he'll never forget. He's an idle loafer...

Jack creeps across stage behind her. Finger on lips to the audience for them to say nothing

Have you seen him? Have you?

Hopefully they say nothing or deny everything

Well?

Jack creeps across the stage the other way but hesitates behind her. She instinctively is aware and turns slowly, he turns with her

Jack, is that you? (*She peers right and left*)

Jack mimes to the audience that he might kick her backside. Hopefully they encourage him but as he goes to do it, Mother turns, and faces him

Aha! (*She makes to grab him*)

Jack's off down the aisle pursued by his mother

                            CURTAIN

ACT II

Scene 1

A Street. In front of the main tabs

Tink makes an entrance. Perhaps dropping his bells again as he does. Then he "sees" the audience and pulls himself together

Tink (*ringing*) Oyez! (*Ringing*) Oyez! (*Ringing*) Oyez! (*Pause then ringing*) Oyez! (*Pause*) I haven't got anything to proclaim. I'm proclaimless. Nothing. Not even one teeny-weeny proclamation. I know what you're thinking — you're all thinking "he's forgotten it", or "he's lost it again". But I haven't. There are no proclamations — big ones (*ringing large bell*) or small ones (*ringing small bell*). I've got nothing to shout about — nowt to shout out about. I'm redundant — they'll give me the sack I suppose. You see now that the Emperor has a birthday celebration *every* Friday — and of course it's a public holiday. Everyone remembers it — I don't need to tell them. Oh, I could tell you about Jack's mother. After she came in shouting and gave everyone a walloping with her broom, well, she was put in the stocks, down on the green, and people all threw rotten apples and tomatoes at her. She wasn't very happy about that — we all laughed, but she didn't. Oh, and Abi, my daughter, is still hiding from the Guard — because of that forged banknote business — when she goes out she has to be in disguise. She can't afford to be recognized.

Jack looks on to the stage. He is furtive

Jack Hey! Hey! Psst! Hey! Is it safe?
Tink What?
Jack (*coming to Tink*) Is it safe?
Tink Abi! (*To audience*) I told you she was good at disguises.
Jack Who is?
Tink You are, Abi.
Jack No, I'm not.
Tink What d'you mean?
Jack I'm not Abi. I'm Jack — the one who sold the cow.
Tink (*with realization*) Jack! Of course it's you — I see that now.

Act II, Scene 1

Jack Have you seen my mother?
Tink Not since you were throwing tomatoes at her in the stocks.
Jack She's looking for me.
Tink I'm not at all surprised.
Jack If she catches me, I shall be in deep trouble. She's never got over those beans.
Tink I have the same problem — it's wind. Beans do it all the time... and rhubarb, it's embarrassing.
Jack I had five of these magic beans and she's gone and thrown them away.
Tink Magic beans?
Jack Five. In exchange for Milky White.
Tink No wonder your mother's upset.
Mother (*off*) Jack! Jack! Where are you? Where are you skulking, you simpleton? Jack! I want a serious word with you. Do you hear me? Jack!
Jack Oh, heck. Oh, lummy! It's her, she's coming this way. I'd better make myself scarce. You won't tell her you've seen me, will you?
Tink Why should I?

Jack goes with a "thanks" through the audience

What will I say?
Mother (*off*) Jack! Is that you? Jack! Jack!

Mother runs in, angry and bespattered with tomato

You're not Jack.
Tink Is that you, Abi? What a disguise.
Mother Have you seen him? Has he been here?
Tink Who do you mean, Abi? (*He knows it's not really her*)
Mother (*giving Tink a cuff*) Stop that! You know very well who I am! Now answer me — have you see my Jack?
Tink Doing what?

She cuffs him again

Ow! That hurts.
Mother And you'll get another if you don't answer me. Have you seen Jack?
Tink I saw him throwing tomatoes at you.
Mother And he'll suffer for it, treating his mother in that way. Not content with selling our cow for a worthless amount.

Tink Five beans.
Mother How did you know that? He's been here, hasn't he? Well, hasn't he?
Tink He was just passing through.
Mother I'll be passing through him when I get my hands on him. (*She moves into the audience,* SR *aisle, viciously asking the audience as she moves through them:* "*Have you seen our Jack?*", "*Did he come this way?*", "*I'll give him a good hiding when I catch him*", "*Did you see him eh? eh?*" *She must aim to frighten the young audience*)

Mother exits

Tink Isn't she fierce? Poor old Jack.

Abigail enters SR *disguised as a beggar*

Abigail What about me?
Tink Go away you scruffy little beggar.
Abigail What? What did you say?
Tink I've no money for you — I can't help — so go and beg somewhere else, you dirty little urchin.
Abigail But it's me, Father. Abi...
Tink Be on your way, I won't tell you again — I'll call the Guard.
Abigail Father! (*Grabbing him*) Don't you know me?
Tink Why should I know a filthy little — wait a bit — is it you, Abi?
Abigail Of course it is.
Tink (*to audience*) Didn't I tell you she was good at disguises.
Abigail You must help me. The Guard Captain is looking for me everywhere. It's because of these forged banknotes. (*She shows them*)
Tink I know... What can we do?
Abigail Speak to the Emperor.
Tink I hardly know him, we weren't at school together.
Abigail Tell him the truth. Tell him how we were both tricked.

Jack eases on SR

Jack Has she gone?
Tink No, she's here, Jack. (*He indicates Abigail*)
Jack Abi... You look terrible.
Abigail Thanks, Jack, you say the nicest things.
Tink It's a disguise — she's hiding from the Guard.
Jack And I'm hiding from my mother.

Act II, Scene 1   29

Abigail Because of the beans?
Jack Right in one. Do you know I just ran home and in our garden there's the biggest beanstalk you've ever seen? I reckon it's where Mother threw the beans.
Abigail She'll be pleased. You'll have beans to eat.
Jack No, she won't. Because they're growing just where her favourite sunflowers should be. She'll be angrier than ever.
Mother (*off*) Jack! Jack! What's happened to my sunflowers?
Jack ⎫
Abigail ⎬ (*together*) Oh! Oh!
Tink ⎭
Tink You'd better run off and hide.
Jack All this running is wearing me out.
Mother (*off*) Jack! You're really in for it this time.
Jack But perhaps you're right.
Abigail Go, Jack. Go. Hide somewhere she'll never think of looking.
Jack (*as he goes via aisle* SR) I'll do my best, Abi. But I don't know where that is. Where could I hide I wonder? Where could I go?

Now hopefully someone in the audience might suggest he climbs the beanstalk, or someone on stage can lead the audience. If not, he'll have to meander out

Tink (*looking offstage* R) I can't see her. But she's out there somewhere.
Abigail I do hope Jack will be safe. (*She looks out front*)

The Guard Captain creeps up behind her and grabs her

Guard Captain Gotcha! You little forger.
Abigail Let me go! Let me go!
Guard Captain You're coming back to the palace with me. I want to introduce you to a dungeon — you'll be there some time.
Abigail Father! Help me! Tell him what happened! Help me!
Guard Captain (*to Tink*) Are you this creature's father?
Tink (*looking at Abigail and then audience*) I've never seen her before in my life.
Abigail (*aghast*) Father!
Guard Captain Come on — no more time wasting.

He drags her off SL *protesting*

Tink (*to audience*) Yes, I know what you're thinking — you're thinking, "What a fibber... He's telling great big porky pies." But if I'd said I was her father, he might have arrested me as well. This way I can try to get Abi released. I might even get Jack to help me! That's a good idea. We'll go to the palace and explain. I'd better find him first. I wonder what's going on at the palace now anyway.

He ambles out via SR *aisle*

Scene 2

The Palace

Main tab opens. We are in some anteroom of some kind. Abacus is at a desk surrounded by papers, ledgers and documents

Abacus (*picking up a bill*) Oh, no! What's this? Two thousand, six hundred. Argh! (*Picking up another bill*) Eight hundred and twenty-seven! For gloves! Oh, good grief. We'll have no money left. (*Picking up another bill*) One thousand-seven hundred and sixty. It's no good, I can't stand it! I can't go on! The Emperor's spending far too much. It's all these birthdays, all these parades and parties.

Lord Chamberlain enters with more bills

Lord Chamberlain Here's some more bills, Abacus. They need paying.
Abacus *More* bills?
Lord Chamberlain (*reading them*) Six new coach horses — eight thousand and six hundred. For new boots — three hundred and six. New cloaks, with fur trim and jewelled clasps — three thousand, two hundred and ——
Abacus Stop! Stop! That's enough. Well, it's more than enough — it's too much. We just don't have the money. The cupboard is bare. The treasury is empty. The vaults have been cleared out.
Lord Chamberlain And all this money is owed to "Trust and Promise", Suppliers to the Royal Household.
Abacus "Trust and Promise" — it's those two "special advisers" to the Emperor. I don't trust them at all, I promise you that!
Lord Chamberlain Surely you don't think they could be tricksters of some kind, do you?
Abacus I wouldn't be surprised.
Lord Chamberlain What can we do about it?

The Emperor enters followed by Sly, Wily and the Empress

Act II, Scene 2

Emperor You're right! You're so right, Lord Trust.
Lord Chamberlain }
Abacus } (*astounded*; *together*) *Lord* Trust!?
Emperor I couldn't possibly wear this old thing again. It's out of the question.
Abacus But it suits you, Sire.
Lord Chamberlain You've never looked so good.
Abacus The country has commented how smart, elegant...
Lord Chamberlain Sophisticated and suave you look.
Sly Don't believe a word of it, Sire.
Abacus They said how... how...
Sly How you couldn't possibly wear it again.
Wily That old thing — they said.
Emperor Did they call me that?
Sly Our Emperor deserves better.
Wily Another birthday parade, another outfit.
Sly Our Emperor should always have the best, the newest, the ——
Wily — crème de la crème.
Emperor Should I?
Sly Because an Emperor who dresses to perfection is the most handsome.
Wily Debonair...
Sly Spectacular...
Wily And above all intelligent, far-sighted, acute, brilliant, brainy, masterful, commanding, superior...
Sly Emperor in the world.
Wily Accompanied as ever by his equally talented and gifted ——
Sly — and breathtakingly beautiful ——
Empress Wife! And I want some more jewels.
Emperor But... Of course.
Sly Leave it to us.
Emperor Now what about plans for this week's birthday? It's already agreed that I need a new outfit.
Lord Chamberlain }
Abacus } (*together*) Oh, no!
Emperor Oh, yes! Oh, yes indeed! What have you in mind, Lord Trust? Lady Promise?
Sly We have a fashion show for you, Sire.
Wily So that you can pick something different.
Sly Something... eye-catching.
Emperor Marvellous! Marvellous! What a super idea — a fashion show. I like it.
Sly Take a seat, Sire!

A catwalk and entrance are set up or disclosed and the onstage cast arrange themselves for the show. "Fashion Show" music pervades the air. Sly and Wily act as the compères

Wily And welcome to this unique display of all that is finest in the fashion world.
Sly As befits our noble benefactor, his royal Highness — the Emperor...
Emperor That's me.
Sly Persimmon.
Emperor That's me too!
Wily Indeed it is, your Highness.
Sly Firstly we have for you, Sire, an exquisite little number. Beautifully cut and styled. You will note the hand-stitching, the delicate embroidery and the overall perfection of the outfit as modelled here today by Vivien.

The Guard Captain and Abigail come in. She struggles

Note the clever use of accessories.
Guard Captain Your Highness. (*A stiff bow*) Keep still you little bratling!
Emperor Is this really me, Lord Trust?
Guard Captain No. It's me, Sire. The Guard Captain.
Sly (*to Wily*) Where did he come from?
Wily I've no idea.
Emperor It doesn't look very stylish or smart.
Empress It's the Guard Captain, Persimmon.
Emperor Do you know, my dear? I think you're right. How long has he been a fashion model?
Guard Captain I've arrested this peasant.
Abigail Let me go, you stupid man. It's all a misunderstanding.
Emperor Will he do a twirl? I need to see it from the back.
Sly Stop! No more. Sire, this is not one of our models.
Wily Not ours.
Emperor Whose is it then?
Empress Come over here, Guard Captain, and bring the peasant with you.
Abigail I had nothing to do with forged money.
Guard Captain Be quiet. Come over here.

They become part of the onstage audience

Empress We'll deal with you later.

Act II, Scene 2   33

Emperor I didn't like that outfit at all. I need something a bit more "me", something that doesn't look as scruffy and second-hand.
Guard Captain What's going on here?
Lord Chamberlain The Emperor's spending more money.
Abacus That we haven't got!
Sly Quiet! Silence!
Wily Ssh! Ssh!
Sly Your Highness. Sorry about that little snag.
Abigail I'm not a little snag!
Guard Captain Quiet.
Sly We have for you that first exquisite little number beautifully cut and styled with, as I said before, the hand-stitching, and all the delicate embroidery work, a truly outstanding outfit as modelled here.

A male model enters wearing an outrageous outfit at which the audience hopefully will laugh, he poses and exits

Wily A reasonably priced ensemble there. Only six thousand, five hundred pounds.
Lord Chamberlain What?
Abacus How much?
Sly Very much in demand these days, Sire?
Wily What's your opinion, great Emperor?
Emperor Who was that?
Sly A model, Sire.
Emperor A model what?
Sly A fashion model, showing the outfit you might wear.
Wily For your next birthday parade.
Emperor You mean I could wear — that?
Sly Oh, yes.
Wily Certainly.
Lord Chamberlain Oh, no.
Abacus Certainly not.

An ad-lib argument between all onstage about the outfit

Empress QUIET!

The noise subsides

   Show us another.
Sly Willingly, your Majesty.

Wily Now we have for you an intriguing and truly unique outfit, cleverly cut and fitted, with a subtlety of colours and materials as befits an Emperor of your standing ——
Emperor — But I'm sitting down.
Sly Even better.

An even more outrageous outfit is modelled on

And at only twelve thousand, nine hundred pounds. I'm sure you will agree that this is a most desirable outfit.
Abacus How much!

Again when the outfit comes on it prompts laughter, the model poses and exits

Emperor Could I wear that?
Abacus No, Sire. No, Sire. No... No... No...
Sly Just imagine yourself in it, Sire.
Wily All heads will turn.
Sly You will be the focus of all attention.
Emperor I will? Do you know — I'm tempted?
Abacus Fight it, your Highness, fight it.
Emperor Let us see it again.
Sly Could we see that distinguished outfit once again?
Wily So elegant. So chic. Quiet please!
Sly Picture yourself like this, your Majesty.

Jack's mother storms on with a rolling pin

Mother I've come for my boy!

Onstage there is an intake of breath from everyone — it is disbelief!

Pause

Emperor Oh, no! Not this one! No, this is not my style at all — I really wouldn't be seen dead wearing this. I mean it actually looks as though things had been thrown together. In fact it looks as though it's had things thrown at it! Tomatoes by the look and by the smell. I mean it's shapeless, isn't it? Baggy. Saggy and baggy — it's like a badly-made bed. It's like a sack of potatoes or a bag of chisels — it really is the most gruesome and unattractive thing I've ever seen. And the model... Well... What can one say. It's beyond a joke. The hair

Act II, Scene 2

resembles a bird's nest and the face. The face is like a bulldog chewing a wasp. Haven't I seen it somewhere before?

During this speech everyone onstage, except the Emperor sees Jack's mother gathering rage. They all back away from what they anticipate is going to be an explosion

Mother (*the explosion*) Aaargghh!

All but the Emperor scuttle away, Abigail, a little less willingly but helped by the Guard Captain

Emperor And I'm sure, I've heard that sound somewhere.
Mother You blot! You spot! You insulting clot.
Emperor Poetic... somewhat.
Mother Have you seen my son, Jack? Speak before I use my rolling pin on you and turn you into piecrust.
Emperor Do you know who I am?
Mother I'll flatten you.
Emperor Tell her, Lord Chamberlain... (*No reply*) Lord Chamberlain... (*Turning and realizing he is alone*) Lord Trust... Abacus... Captain of the Guard... Where are you all?
Mother Never mind them. Have... you... seen... my... Jack...?
Emperor (*now scared*) Jack? No... Now listen, my good woman.
Mother I'm nobody's good woman. (*She advances towards him*)
Emperor Keep away. (*He backs into the audience area*)
Mother (*following him but at the opposite side of the audience*) If you're the Emperor you can find my son for me.
Emperor I wouldn't know where to look.
Mother Order someone to do it. You're in charge.
Emperor What do you mean *tell* someone?
Mother What are you? A man or a mouse?
Emperor I'm neither. I'm an emperor... a ruler.
Mother Well, start ruling or do you want me to come over there and give you a few reminders? (*She waves the rolling pin menacingly*)
Emperor I'll do it! Don't come near me with that thing (*Turning to adjacent members of the audience*) She shouldn't speak to me like that... I'm the Emperor.
Mother What did you say?
Emperor I was just asking if anyone had seen your son — er — er — Fred.
Mother Jack! Jack! Can't you get anything right? (*Coming round the front of the audience towards him*) Perhaps I can give you a little encouragement.

Emperor (*backing away*) No... Keep away. I bruise very easily. I'm delicate. I've got a cough... and weak ankles. Keep away.
Mother (*getting closer*) Who's got a face like a bulldog?
Emperor Did I say that? No, I didn't mean a bulldog. A face like a... like a...

She is very close now

Mother Well?
Emperor A warthog!

He runs out of the auditorium

Mother Aaarggh! What! Come back here!

She follows him off

Sly and Wily return warily to the stage

Sly Where did she come from?
Wily Where's she gone to?
Sly She could cause us trouble, we need to take what we've got and move on.
Wily No! No! We can do better yet. There's more tricks we can play to get money out of this stupid Emperor.
Sly Like what?
Wily Well, we can sell him more clothes. He believes anything.
Sly Where can we get more clothes? We've sold him virtually all we could lay our hands on.
Wily So what have we got to sell him?
Sly Nothing.

Pause

Wily That's it. We'll sell him nothing and he'll think it's everything.
Sly Explain.
Wily Listen. It's like this...

They make to go into a huddle

   The Empress returns

Act II, Scene 2   37

Empress Who is that dreadful woman? She storms around the place like a whirlwind, threatening everybody and everything. And where's Persimmon?
Sly I think he might be trying to reason with her, your Highness.
Mother (*off*) Even if you are Emperor you're not too big to smack!
Emperor (*off*) No... No... Don't touch me!
Wily Yes. That seems to be the case.
Empress He's useless, completely useless. I should never have married him. I was meant for something better than this. I really was. That husband of mine needs teaching a lesson. I know he's the Emperor but he needs teaching a lesson. I should leave him, move away from this palace. Take what I can and buy me a country of my own. That would show him.
Wily It would be expensive.
Sly Very expensive.
Wily Where would the money come from?
Empress I can't think.
Sly Perhaps we can help, your Highness.
Wily Perhaps you could help us. And in return, we ——
Sly — could help you.

Pause

Empress What have you in mind?
Wily We have a plan, your Highness.
Sly Which would make us all richer, your Highness.
Empress Call me Petronella.

They make a huddle, lots of whispers, a pause then laughter

Yes! Yes! I like it... I love it... Do it! We'll do it! Oh yes! It will serve him right...Oh, yes! Yes!
Sly Let's go and discuss the finer points.
Wily The share out.
Empress You really are "special advisers", aren't you?
Sly We certainly are.
Sly
Wily } (*together*) Petronella!

They exit SR

Tink and Jack appear on the catwalk

Tink You shouldn't be climbing trees at your age, Jack.
Jack It's a beanstalk, not a tree.
Tink Well, it's big enough to be a tree. In fact it's big enough to be ten trees. It's so high. Whatever will your mother say?
Jack Who's going to tell her? She'll never realize.
Tink Anyway, Jack, now we're here at the palace we need to find Abi.
Jack Do you know the Emperor's Court?
Tink I didn't even know he'd escaped.
Jack No. I meant the court at the palace. Do you know where Abi might be?
Tink The dungeon — she'll be in a dungeon I suppose — and we'll have to overpower the guards, and take the keys, or we may have to break down the doors ourselves and bend the iron bars and ——
Jack — Couldn't we just pay a fine?
Tink Pay a fine? Pay a fine? Oh, that's great coming from you. You who had to sell the cow because you'd no money and I've no money. So what will we pay the fine with? Buttons?
Jack Gold.
Tink Gold? Of course, why didn't I think about that? Gold! Yes! There's just one problem — we don't have any.
Jack I do.
Tink So now, let's see if we can find some weapons and some... What did you say?
Jack I said "I do". I've got gold. Look. (*And from a knapsack or his pockets, he produces several bags of gold*)
Tink (*astounded*) But... It is gold. Bags of gold. Where on earth did this all come from?
Jack Up the beanstalk.
Tink Up the... Oh, yes. Of course it did, I don't think. Whose is it?
Jack Mine. Ours now.
Tink What do you mean "now"? Whose was it?
Jack I took it from the Ogre who lives ——
Tink — at the top of the beanstalk, I suppose.
Jack How did you know?
Tink Oh, never mind. You can tell me the truth later. Let's go and find Abi and get her out of prison.

Sly, Wily and the Empress enter giggling, laughing and shaking hands

Empress Wait! Stay! What are you two peasants doing here?
Tink (*a low bow*) Your Majesty, I am the Town Crier.

Act II, Scene 2   39

Empress I know what you are but what are you doing — here — in the royal palace?
Jack Your Majesty, we're here to pay the fine so that Abigail Bell can be released from imprisonment.
Empress Fine? (*Bewildered*) Fine?
Tink She was caught in possession of forged money, your Majesty.
Sly Disgraceful!
Wily Dastardly!
Sly Keep her locked up!
Wily Forever and ever!
Sly Amen.
Jack And we've brought gold to pay her fine.
Sly Gold?
Wily Gold?
Empress Gold?

Abacus appears

Abacus Gold?

The Lord Chamberlain appears

Lord Chamberlain Did you say?
All (*except Tink and Jack*; *together*) GOLD?
Jack How many pieces will it cost?
Sly No pieces.
Wily Just bagfuls.

Sly and Wily take the bags

Jack Hey!
Tink That seems a big fine!
Empress Prices have just gone up — inflation! (*Taking the bags from Sly and Wily*)

The Lord Chamberlain helps the Empress

Abacus And so have taxes.
Sly ⎫
Wily ⎭ (*together*) Hey!
Empress Put it in the treasury, Abacus. The Emperor might want to buy some new clothes.
Sly Oh, yes. I'm sure he will.

Wily I think he will.
Empress I know he will.
Tink So will you release her now then?
Empress Only when the fine is paid.
Jack That was the fine.
Empress No, that was taxes. You have to find more gold for the fine.
Tink And where will we do that?
Jack I know, Tink. Leave it to me!

He runs off through the audience

The Emperor appears on the catwalk, somewhat dishevelled

Empress Persimmon!
Sly
Wily } (*together*) Your Highness.
Abacus Sire!
Lord Chamberlain You look worn out.
Emperor That's because I am worn out. I've been chased round the city by that lunatic woman with a rolling pin. I am absolutely tired out. She was threatening me all the time and I thought that any minute she would catch me and ooh! I don't like to think about it.
Empress Persimmon, forget all that, for we have the most astounding news. Is that not true, Lord Trust?
Sly It is indeed, your Majesty. You will be completely overwhelmed — over-awed...
Wily Gobsmacked, Sire.
Tink What about my daughter?
Empress Later, peasant, later — when you have more gold.
Emperor What is it? I need cheering up. I need something to lift my spirits — is it exciting?
Sly It is indeed.
Emperor Will I be thrilled?
Wily You most certainly will.
Emperor Can I eat it?
Empress No, Persimmon. It's far... far... far better than that.
Emperor Can I ride it?
Wily No, Sire.
Emperor What then? What? Tell me what.
Sly Lord Emperor, we have long been trying to find a new and outstanding outfit for you to wear on your next birthday parade, have we not?
Emperor Oh, it's not more of the fashion show, is it? I think I've seen enough of that.

Act II, Scene 2

Empress It's not that.
Wily No more fashion show.
Sly Sire, we have discovered a brand new material the like of which you will never have seen before. The colours and patterns are exquisite, the texture, the feel of it is beyond belief.
Wily But it has a quality that no other material in the world has.
Emperor And what is that?
Sly To people who are unintelligent, who have no thinking power — people who are in the wrong job, people who cannot be trusted, people who are — nobody. This material is ——
Wily — invisible.
Sly But if you are intelligent, clever, trustworthy, and in the right job then you will see the wonderful colours and patterns.
Emperor Let me have a look at this amazing material. You have some to show us?
Wily Oh, yes. Yes indeed. Lord Trust, bring the material.

Sly exits and returns remarkably quickly with a roll of this invisible cloth

Sly Here it is, your Highness.
Wily Unroll it.

Sly does

Ah! Now look at that...
Empress Such colours... Such patterns...
Sly What do you think, Sire?
Emperor I'm not sure.
Wily What?
Sly If you are intelligent and in the right job then...
Emperor Oh, yes! I see the colours now. Aren't they so... so...?
Empress Vibrant.
Emperor Are they? I mean... Yes, and purple always was my favourite colour.
Empress Blue.
Emperor That's what I meant. What do you think, Chamberlain?
Lord Chamberlain Well, Sire. I must say that I can't see...
Wily Only the wisest, cleverest Chamberlains can actually see the quality of the material. If you are a dimwit and not fit to be Lord Chamberlain then you see nothing.
Lord Chamberlain It's beautiful.
Sly And so reasonably priced — one hundred gold pieces per yard.

Abacus How much?
Sly A bargain price...
Abacus But there's nothing...
Sly Only a real, qualified, intelligent treasurer can recognize the exquisite value of the material.
Abacus But there's nothing.
Emperor What?
Abacus Nothing... that I can add, the material is worth every...penny.
Wily Every gold piece, do you mean?
Abacus I'm afraid I do.
Tink Just a minute. I might be wrong but you say this material——
Sly Careful, don't stand on it.
Tink Eh?
Wily And don't handle it too roughly. Are your hands clean?
Tink But——
Empress Loyal citizens who want to get their daughters out of prison can see the quality of this material almost at once.
Tink (*handling the material*) Isn't it soft? Isn't it so very... soft? You hardly know you're touching anything at all.
Emperor I must have it. I want it. I'll have an outfit made from it. It's — incredible.
Sly Isn't it just?
Wily But it is most expensive as you might expect.
Emperor I don't care how much it costs — I *will* have it. Get me this material! Make me this outfit with two pairs of trousers, then everyone will know how intelligent and clever I am, won't they?
Empress They will indeed, Persimmon. They will indeed.
Emperor If it costs more gold then I'll get more gold. Where will it come from, Abacus?
Abacus More taxes ...
Emperor From my adoring subjects, they can hardly wait to pay. And once they see what they've paid for they will be speechless.
Sly You can be sure of that, Sire.
Emperor Measure me! I need to be measured! I shall look splendid, shall I not?
Wily I can honestly say, Sire, that when you wear this suit ——
Sly — all eyes will be upon you.
Empress People will say "I've never seen anything like that".
Emperor Let me be measured! Let me be measured!

Sly, Wily and the Empress busy themselves with this task. Abacus and the Lord Chamberlain talk animatedly albeit very quietly about cash flows and the like

Tink When can I get my daughter back? Where's Abi? That's what I came for. (*Calling*) Abi! Abi!
Mother (*off*) Jack! Jack! Jack!

All onstage freeze, then move very deliberately and exit. The Emperor goes last, choosing to go SL *and then changing his mind to go* SR. *As he creeps warily* SR *feeling he is safe, Jack's mother is there and chases him round stage and off* SR, *after one or two circuits, with ad-lib dialogue*

(*To the audience*) If he's the Emperor, I'm a Dutchman. Weed! Wimp! He needs a good hiding. Like my Jack, when I catch him. That's not you, Jack, is it? Sitting there... Let me have a closer look... (*She moves into the aisle*)

The main CURTAIN *closes*

Jack enters down the other aisle

Jack Tink! Tink! We're saved, I've got some more... Just wait till you see what I have in this sack, Tink!
Mother Jack!
Jack Mother!

A chase ensues across stage using the exit doors on the proscenium arch and the main curtain. Finally Jack's Mother believes she knows where he is behind the main curtain because of the "bumps" in the curtain. She lines herself up for a good thump with her rolling pin. Thwack! There is a suitably large groan backstage

The Emperor staggers through the main tab, clutching his head and collapses

Mother (*to the collapsed figure*) That's not my Jack!!

CURTAIN

ACT III

Scene 1

A Street

In front of the main curtain. Tink makes a somewhat reluctant entrance from either side. He eventually positions himself somewhat centrally

Tink Ding-a-ling! Ding! Ding! Oyez! Ding-a-ling! Ding! Ding! Ding! Oyez! Ding-a-ling. Oh, bubbles! I know what you're thinking — you're thinking he's gone and forgotten his bell now or he's lost it. Well, it's not true. It's been taken away from me. It's been commandeered. The Great Lord Chamberpot. I mean Lord Chamberlain and that Abacus Treasurer have taken everything that is metal — just in case it's gold. The country is so short of money. This new suit of clothes for the Emperor is costing arms and legs. And I need some gold to pay the fine so that Abi can get out of prison. I wish Jack would come back with some more.

Jack runs down the aisle SL

Jack Tink! Tink! I'm back.
Tink How did I do that? Do you think I've got two more wishes? Have you got the gold?
Jack Yes and no.
Tink What do you mean? Yes and no.
Jack Listen... I went back home and climbed the beanstalk. It really is so very tall.
Tink (*to the audience*) He's got a wonderful imagination.
Jack And I went into the Ogre's castle.
Tink At the top of the beanstalk? (*He indicates he doubts Jack's sanity*)
Jack That's right and he wasn't about.
Tink You'd have noticed him if he was.
Jack You're right I would. So I crept into the kitchen and pinched his ——
Tink —— bottom?

Act III, Scene 1

Jack — his hen. His speckled hen and I put it in a sack and came back down the ——
Tink — Beanstalk?
Jack Yes, and I came up to the palace to meet you.
Tink With a hen?
Jack Ingrid.
Tink You brought a hen... but no gold?
Jack No! This is the amazing bit. The hen lays golden eggs...
Tink Do you know I worry about you, Jack? I think you've been out in the sun. Perhaps you should lie down. (*To the audience*) He never was very bright. Magic beans, beanstalks, ogres, golden eggs...
Jack (*showing a golden egg*) Like this one.
Tink (*to the audience*) Like that one. (*Double take*) Let me see. (*Taking the egg*) It is gold. It's a golden egg... Real gold... Pure gold... Look! Look! (*Showing it to some of the audience*) Gold! We're rich! We're rich! Jack, you are a genius. I believe every word you say. Golden eggs. Wow!

He almost dances onto stage and throws the egg to Jack who throws it back to him. Ad-lib dialogue during this

Abacus enters and watches this for a while

Abacus (*moving in and catching the egg*) Taxes! Needy case! The Emperor's needs are greater than yours.

He exits

Tink Hey! That's not right! That's not fair! That's ours. Our egg. Ingrid gave it to us, she... Just a second... Jack.
Jack What? What now?
Tink Get her to lay another.
Jack I can't.
Tink Talk nicely to her. Make noises like chickenfeed.
Jack I can't do it. I haven't got her any more.
Tink Don't tell me the Ogre came down the beanstalk and took her back.
Jack No, the Chamberlain confiscated her to pay for ——
Tink — taxes! I might have guessed. So we've no gold.
Jack Not any more.
Tink Get back up the beanstalk. Try again.
Jack I thought you didn't believe in my beanstalk.

Tink Me? Not believe? Ha! Ha! Go on, get a move on. Have another climb.
Jack Right! I will. I will.
Tink Don't be too long.
Jack Back as soon as I can.

He exits via SR *aisle*

Tink I don't know where he's *really* getting the gold from but it's worth a try.

The Guard Captain enters with collecting boxes

Guard Captain You there... Peasant...
Tink You mean me?
Guard Captain Would you care to make a donation to the New Clothes for the Emperor Fund?
Tink No, I would not.
Guard Captain (*grabbing Tink*) Let me put that another way. You *would* like to make a donation to the New Clothes for the Emperor Fund, wouldn't you?
Tink Yes! Yes! Now you've explained what a good cause it is. Would you like a button or a bit of silver paper?
Guard Captain Cash? Gold?

Tink shrugs a shrug that tells all

We need all the money we can get. His outfit is going to be so expensive.
Tink Have you seen it?
Guard Captain (*warying*) No! ... I mean "yes". I've ...er ... seen the material, have you?
Tink The material? Oh, yes. Such a lovely colour.
Guard Captain ⎫ (*together*) ⎧ Green!
Tink ⎭ ⎩ Red!
Guard Captain ⎫ (*together*) Magnificent.
Tink ⎭
Guard Captain Help me collect. You take that side. I'll do this. (*He gives Tink a collecting box*)

Act III, Scene 2   47

They move through the audience trying to obtain donations. Ad-lib dialogue, "Worthy cause", "New Clothes for the Emperor", "Spare a gold piece or two", etc. Any member of the audience who protests "There's nothing there" should be told "Well, you're not very intelligent are you", etc. If the going becomes too tough they should not dwell long among the audience

Main CURTAIN *opens*

SCENE 2

The Palace Again!

The Emperor's head is bandaged and he is being tended by Abigail. The Empress, Sly and Wily are in attendance too

Emperor Ow! Ouch! Ooh! Ouch! Ouch! Oooh! Ow! Be careful. I'm fragile.
Abigail I'm being as gentle as I can be, your Majesty.
Emperor I was hit on the head you know.
Abigail So I believe.
Emperor Some vicious thug hit me when I wasn't looking. Ow! You're not being careful enough. Ow!
Empress Watch what you're doing, peasant!
Abigail I'm not a nurse.
Empress You are now — we can't afford to employ a real nurse.
Sly Is it any easier, Sire?
Emperor No, it is not.
Wily And you've been so brave about it too.
Emperor Brave? Yes, I have, haven't I? Ow! That smarts.
Abigail Sorry! But if you won't keep still I can't help it.
Empress Cheeky little peasant.
Abigail I really am doing my best.
Empress (*forcefully*) Don't raise your voice to me, you drab.
Emperor Stop! Stop! My head! My head! It's aching again. I'm feeling limp again. I... might... even... faint...
Empress Oh, do pull yourself together, Persimmon.
Sly Remember your birthday, Sire.
Wily All the celebrations, the parade, the procession.
Emperor (*hazily but feigned*) Birthday? Celebrations? Parade? I don't remember.
Empress (*to Abigail*) Have you tied those bandages too tightly?
Abigail No! Of course I haven't. (*Sotto voce*) Not tightly enough!

Empress What?
Abigail Nothing!
Sly Sire, this Friday, as indeed every Friday. It's your birthday.
Emperor Is it? My birth — day.
Wily With a parade and bands and drums and bagpipes and ——
Emperor I remember. Yes. I do recall. It's coming back to me.
Sly Thank goodness!
Emperor But I — I — I'm not going. No. Cancel it! I can't possibly go. I'm far too feeble. My head won't stand the noise. Cancel it. Cancel all the arrangements. It may even be that I — I — won't — have — any more — birthday parades.
Sly Oh, Sire. Don't say that.
Wily Please don't talk that way.
Empress You *must* celebrate, Persimmon.

The Emperor coughs for sympathy and groans a bit as Abigail tends the bandage. Sly, Wily and the Empress huddle briefly — what can they do about it?

Sly (*inspiration*) But Sir! What about your new clothes?
Wily Your astounding new clothes.
Empress Your unique new clothes... like no others in the world.

Pause

Sly Your country expects.

Pause

Emperor (*a little cough*) Unique?
Sly The most unique.
Wily Perhaps you'd like to try the jacket on.
Emperor (*suddenly alert*) Could I?
Wily Is it ready, Lord Trust?
Sly I'll go get it... and the cloak too.

He exits

Emperor The cloak too? I'm feeling better already.
Empress Such fortitude, Persimmon... How do you do it?
Emperor It's something we emperors have built in.

Sly enters with an empty coat hanger

Act III, Scene 2

Sly Ta-da! How about that, your Majesty?
Emperor Er...
Wily Before you speak, Sire. Let me remind you that there are people in the world who are so dim, so stupid, so thick, so half-witted, so unintelligent that they cannot see this beautiful material.
Emperor Really?
Abigail Yes, but ——
Empress (*grabbing Abigail and half gagging her*) — and can I remind you that there are peasants who will rot forever in the deepest dungeon if they open their mouths to say anything about this absolutely wonderful outfit. You understand?

Abigail nods

Emperor It's — superb. It's — splendid. Truly, truly the finest I've ever seen. Let me try it on. (*He grabs at the "jacket"*)
Sly Careful, Sire. Watch out for the embroidery.
Emperor What? Oh, yes. Of course. Help me! Help me!

Sly and Wily help the Emperor into his "jacket" — he may need to remove the one he has on

Wily Careful, Sire, careful.
Emperor I can't find the sleeve. Help me find the sleeve.
Sly Gently. Here. Just straighten the collar.
Emperor What?
Wily I'll do it... There... A beautiful fit.
Sly Do you want to try it with the buttons fastened?
Emperor Buttons?
Sly The ruby and diamond buttons.
Emperor Oh, those buttons. No. No, I like it open. (*To the Empress*) What do you think my dear?
Empress It's definitely you, Persimmon. Just do a turn.

The Emperor does

  So elegant. Perfect...
Emperor It's so light and comfortable — I'd hardly know I had it on. Great Scott! I've just had the most brilliant idea!
Wily Tell us, my Lord.
Emperor (*to the Empress*) You too will have an outfit made from this astounding material and you will wear it in the parade alongside me. What do you say to that?

Abigail Great idea! Do it!
Empress (*thumping Abigail*) Who asked for your opinion?
Sly But, Sire. The expense...
Wily The cost would be double at least.

They are rubbing their hands with glee

Emperor No matter. My wife is worth it. What do you say, my dear?

Pause

Empress You're so kind, Persimmon, but it is *your* birthday. I think it only right that nothing and no one, not even I, should detract from you on that day. All eyes *must* be on you.
Emperor (*pause*) You're right! As ever. Let me try the cloak.

Sly and Wily do the honours

Sly Just turn away, your Majesty, while I fix the shoulder clasps. There...
Wily And the train falls nicely at the back right out to here. As you can see...
Emperor To where?
Wily (*indicating*) To here, your Highness.

Abacus and Lord Chamberlain enter, swiftly

Abacus Your Majesty, we must speak about the expenditure.
Lord Chamberlain We are vastly overspent, your Highness.
Emperor Don't step on my train.
Abacus What?
Lord Chamberlain Train?
Sly You came just at the right moment, my Lords. The Emperor is trying on his jacket and cloak.
Wily For the parade... The grand procession...
Empress His splendid new outfit — you remember?
Abacus Oh yes *that* one!
Lord Chamberlain We remember!
Emperor Isn't it something else?
Abacus Isn't it just. But Sire... The cost... The country is bankrupt. We haven't a bean.
Wily (*with an eye to the main chance*) Do you want to buy some beans?

Act III, Scene 2   51

Lord Chamberlain All the gold we had collected in taxes has gone.
Abacus And that hen that lays the golden eggs...
Lord Chamberlain She can't keep up. She's three behind already.
Sly We had to pay for the material, Sire.
Wily And the tailors and the seamstresses...
Sly Buttonholers...
Wily Embroiderers...
Emperor Stop! No more of this! It's worth it. I will be remembered forever in this outfit. I can hardly wait for it to be completed. I shall be — I shall be — what shall I be?
Sly Someone might write a story about you.
Wily You'd be immortalized.
Emperor You bet I would! I need to see myself. I need to see how I look. Let's go and look in a mirror. Chamberlain, Abacus, Trust, Promise, pick up the train.
Wily What?
Emperor We don't want it to get dirty, do we? Come! My dear, take my arm.

The Empress does

Watch out for the cuff. The embroidery is so delicate. Peasant, you can come too.

The invisible train is picked up and the entourage moves off

Come along. I can hardly wait for the parade. Lift the train higher, Abacus. Don't pull on it. It hurts my shoulders. Come along. Come along.

They go

The main Tabs close

Tink enters down aisle SL

Tink (*rattling his tin*) Your last chance, oyez! Your very last chance to make a contribution to this worthwhile cause. New clothes for the Emperor! Anybody like to contribute anything more? I'm not doing very well. Most people say they've given enough already. Some people said "let him do without" but you can't do without clothes, can you? I wonder how much I've collected. Perhaps I'll just open my tin and have a look — a quick count up. I can always put it back, can't I? Let's have a look.

Tink moves onto stage and opens the collecting box. Its paltry contents fall onto the stage

That's not much, is it? Some buttons and some foreign coins (*this would be sterling of course*) and look, some of those forged banknotes. Now who put those in? I should be able to remember.

The Guard Captain enters. He is struggling to open his collecting tin

Guard Captain Aha! What are you doing?
Tink What are *you* doing?
Guard Captain I asked first. Have you opened your collecting tin?
Tink (*mock surprise*) Oh... It's open. How did that happen? The bottom must have fallen off . I never realized and all the money has dropped out. What a thing to happen.
Guard Captain (*shaking his tin*) I wish my bottom would fall off.
Tink (*pause*) What? Pardon?
Guard Captain Then I could see how much I've collected.
Tink Oh... The tin... I see. Well, you have to help it fall off. Let me show you. You see it's this little flap here. You just encourage it to open. (*Groaning a little as he does this*) And lo and behold. We're open for business.
Guard Captain So how much have I collected?
Tink (*shaking it out*) About as much as I have.
Guard Captain Is that gold there?
Tink No, it's a bottle top and look — you've got some forged banknotes too.
Guard Captain Anyone caught with forged banknotes has to go to prison.
Tink I know. My daughter, Abi, is already there.
Guard Captain So are these yours?
Tink You don't catch me like that. Some of these are yours.

Pause

Tink
Guard Captain } (*grabbing each other; together*) I arrest you!
Tink Wait a minute. That's not right. Someone put these notes in our tins.
Guard Captain Who? I don't remember.
Tink To get rid of them, I'll bet. But who is giving them out? There's some tricksters around, I'm sure of it.

Act III, Scene 2   53

Jack enters down aisle SR, *carrying a sack*

Jack Tink! Here I am again. And wait till you see what I've got this time. What are you doing?

Tink collects the money back into the tins with the Guard Captain

Tink Our bottoms dropped off.
Guard Captain We've been collecting for the Emperor's New Clothes Fund.
Tink I hope you've had more success with what you were doing.
Jack Tink, it's fantastic. You'll not believe what I've been up to.
Tink That's true.
Jack I ran straight home from the palace and went up the beanstalk.
Guard Captain You went where?
Tink Up the beanstalk.

The Guard Captain would speak...

Don't ask.
Jack Up and up and up. To the top. To the ——
Tink — the Ogre's Palace.
Guard Captain The what?!
Tink The Ogre's Palace. What else do you get at the top of beanstalks? Ssh!
Jack So I went in and the Ogre was ——
Tink — away on holiday?
Jack No. Asleep... fast asleep... snoring... So very quietly. I went past him and into his library.
Tink I didn't know Ogres had libraries.
Jack It's where he keeps his most precious things.
Guard Captain Like what? Like what precious things?
Jack Like this (*He discloses from the sack or parcel a magnificent gold and bejewelled harp*)
Guard Captain What is it?
Tink What do you mean "what is it"? Can't you see? It's a — a — whatsit —a — precious thing.
Jack It's a harp, Tink, a harp. It's a harp... a harp.
Tink All right. Don't go on about it.
Jack And listen. (*He takes the harp*)

As he touches the strings, music begins. It may be harp music at first but it swells into a full orchestra!

Guard Captain How did you do that?
Tink I didn't know you could even play a precious thing, Jack.
Jack A harp! It's an enchanted harp. It plays itself. It really does.
Tink And it's made of gold too. We'll melt it down and use the gold to pay Abi's fine.
Jack No! It's worth more like this. We'll be able to give concerts, recitals. The world will flock to hear the magic harp.
Guard Captain Won't the — the — Ogre want it back? If it's one of his precious things.
Tink He might miss it.
Jack He won't know where it's gone. He won't know where to look.
Guard Captain He might be a bit angry — upset.
Tink He might search around for it.
Guard Captain Getting angrier and angrier.
Jack No! He won't do that, will he?

Sound FX. Huge roaring voice of the Ogre:
  "Fee-fi-fo-fum, I smell the blood of an Englishman.
  Be he alive or be he dead...
  I'll grind his bones to make my bread."
And he growls loudly. There is a pause. The harp plays menacing music

Tink Is that your mother, Jack?

Jack shakes his head

  Looking for you?

Jack shakes his head

  Are you sure?

Jack nods his head

  Jack's Mother runs in down the aisle SR. *She is speechless*

Jack Mother! Are you all right?

Mother mimes her situation; out of breath, scared and bewildered

Tink What's happened?

Mother mimes the beanstalk, looking up and seeing something big and ugly and fierce

Guard Captain Was that you doing all that shouting, disturbing the peace on the Emperor's birthday?

Mother shakes her head and "explains" again that it is something large and aggressive

Tink She can't speak.
Guard Captain I think she's had a shock!
Jack (*realization*) It's the Ogre. He's coming to get his ——
Tink — precious thing.
Jack — own back. He'll be coming down the beanstalk all angry and...

Mother nods wildly in agreement

Loud Sound FX again:
"Fee-fi-fo-fum, I smell the blood of an Englishman.
Be he alive or be he dead...
I'll grind his bones to make my bread."

Mother collapses, fainting into the arms of the Guard Captain and Tink

Tink And he seems hungry.
Guard Captain What can we do?
Jack Leave it to me. Look after the harp and my mother.

He runs off down an aisle

Tink Look after yourself, Jack! Right then. Let's get on with it.

They let Mother fall and both go for the harp

Tink
Guard Captain } (*together*) I'll get the harp. You look after Jack's mother.

They struggle with the harp. Ad-lib "I'll do this, you look after her", "No, you look after her and I'll take the harp", etc. Eventually they leave the harp and carry on their argument

Mother comes to and picks up the harp. It plays "Happy Birthday to You". Tink and Guard Captain turn and freeze, then break apart

Guard Captain It's the Emperor's birthday!

Tink It's time for the parade!
Guard Captain I should be at the palace!
Tink I must get Abi released!
Guard Captain We don't want to miss this. Come on!

He picks up the collecting tins and exits SL

Tink (*grabbing the harp from Mother*) Wait for me!

He follows the Guard Captain off SL

Mother tries to shout "Hey! Hey! Wait for me!"

Mother (*to the audience*) I've lost my voice, I can't shout! What can I do! (*To the Guard Captain and Tink*) Hey! Hey! Just a minute!

She follows them off SL

Main CURTAIN *opens*

SCENE 3

Town Square bedecked with flags

Abacus and the Lord Chamberlain are on stage, arranging the final parade details

Abacus It's no good complaining to me. If the townspeople won't line the streets, then they won't.
Lord Chamberlain They say it's a public holiday and they'll do what they like.
Abacus But at least we've got all these people over here. (*Indicating the audience*) They look a decent crowd.
Lord Chamberlain Yes, splendid, especially that one. Now where will you be standing?
Abacus Aren't I in the parade?
Lord Chamberlain I thought you could lead the cheers.
Abacus Me?
Lord Chamberlain Be a cheerleader.
Abacus What, me? A cheerleader?
Lord Chamberlain Do your best.

Abacus might "rehearse" a few "cheerleader" moves

Act III, Scene 3

Sly and Wily enter

Sly Where are all the people?
Lord Chamberlain Out there. (*He indicates the audience*)
Wily What about the townspeople?
Lord Chamberlain They'll come out when the Parade arrives. Hopefully...
Sly It will be a sight worth seeing, the Emperor in his brand new ——
Wily Highly expensive...
Sly Unique...
Sly }
Wily } (*together*) Clothes!

They laugh a little together

Lord Chamberlain I've never seen clothes like them.
Sly They are magnificent, aren't they?
Lord Chamberlain Well, er... er...
Wily Such fantastic material that only the most intelligent people appreciate it.
Sly Do you know, Lord Chamberlain, that there are some really brainless, clueless, simpletons in the world who cannot see the beauty and splendour?
Lord Chamberlain Are there? What fools! What idiots! What downright nincompoops...
Abacus (*part of his routine*) Ra! Ra! Ra!

Abigail enters, holding a bandage

Abigail We've got problems. The Emperor's banged his head again on the wardrobe door. He says he can't possibly appear in the parade today. He says the suit will have to go back.
Sly What? Go back?
Wily He's not thinking of refunds, is he?
Sly Don't say that!
Wily (*to Abigail*) I thought you were looking after him.
Abigail I've done my best but he says he needs a lie down.

The Empress enters

Empress Quick! Quick! We need to get him ready for the parade before he really does change his mind. Help me get him into the New Clothes.

Sly Can't you do it?
Wily It's not all that hard surely?
Empress Someone needs to persuade him while others dress him. Come along.

Sly, Wily and the Empress exit

Lord Chamberlain Is his head really bad?
Abigail I don't think it's any worse than usual.
Abacus As bad as that?
Abigail He's playing for sympathy all the time. He's a typical man.
Lord Chamberlain Eh?
Abigail And he believes everything those two and the Empress tell him. Do you know, I don't trust them at all? That Lord Trust and his friend, Lady Promise, look a bit like two no-goods who gave me forged money.
Abacus Some kind of tricksters, do you mean?
Abigail It wouldn't surprise me.

Tink enters with the harp

Abigail Father! Where's your bell? You've forgotten your bell.
Tink It was confiscated. (*Indicating Abacus and the Lord Chamberlain*) They said it could be valuable. Now don't put me off because I'm about to announce the Emperor's Birthday Parade.
Lord Chamberlain The Parade? Will it happen then?
Tink As soon as I've proclaimed it, it will take place.
Lord Chamberlain Good heavens, I'm supposed to be there. I don't want them to start without me.

He dashes off SL

Abacus (*to Abigail*) Right, peasant. You can practise the cheering. You say "Hooray" after three. One... two... three!
Abigail (*wearily*) Hooray.
Abacus No, that's not enthusiastic enough. We need a big cheer for the Emperor. Even three...
Abigail (*indicating the audience*) Ask them?
Abacus Oh, yes. I could. Yes, they could cheer too I suppose. "Hooray" after three, eh? Why not? Here we go. One... two ...

Act III, Scene 3

Sound FX loudest:
  "Fee-fi-fo-fum, I smell the blood of an Englishman,
  Be he alive or be he dead...
  I'll grind his bones to make my bread"

Abacus (*weedily*) Hooray.
Abigail What on earth's that?
Tink It's Jack's ogre. Don't worry, he's dealing with it.
Abigail Ogre? What do you mean ogre?
Tink Big, fierce, ugly, vicious. You know what ogres are.
Abigail Of course I do but where's he come from?
Tink The top of Jack's beanstalk, he says.
Abigail (*thinking*) Yes... Yes... The magic beans. I remember.
Abacus (*pointing out front*) You can just see part of it from here. Look...
Abigail (*looking out front*) Oh, yes. What's that big dark shape?
Tink That'll be the ogre. (*Realizing what he's said*) He's climbing down the — Help! He'll eat us alive.

Sound FX: "Fee-fi-fo-fum". No other line

The stage lights dim, perhaps a shape becomes apparent (a gobo?) across the stage

Abigail What's Jack going to do about it?
Abacus Run away?
Tink Hide? What could he do?
Abigail I don't know. What?

Hopefully the audience might say "chop it down"

Allow a space of time for this to occur to them then Sound FX: chopping increasing in volume

The Lights dim slowly to Black-out which coincides with the sound of a falling beanstalk and shouts from the Ogre. Lights back up full

Abacus, Abigail and Tink are still on stage, turning away, holding their ears and covering their eyes

Pause

  (*Quietly*) He must have chopped it down.

Tink and Abacus nod

Tink No more gold or precious things...
Abigail What do you mean, Father?
Tink I'll explain after the parade. Let me do the proclaiming. (*He plucks the harp*)

A carillon rings out

Oyez! (*He plucks again*)

Another elaborate carillon

(*Addressing the harp*) You don't have to be so flamboyant! Oyez! (*He plucks again*)

A solitary "dong"

Oyez! Now hear this all good townspeople wherever you may be and all you good people out there! Welcome to the Emperor Persimmon's Birthday Parade. Today he celebrates his — (*To Abacus*) What birthday is it?
Abacus This week's.
Tink Today the Emperor celebrates this week's birthday. To mark this special occasion, the Emperor has had made ——
Abacus — at stupendous expense.
Tink — at stupendous expense, a completely New Suit of Clothes. Ladies and gentlepersons — three cheers for his Highness — the Emperor! (*He plucks the harp*)

Triumphant music is heard

Abacus (*calling to the crowd*) Hip! Hip!

The audience may respond

Hip! Hip!

Abigail claps

Hip!

Act III, Scene 3

The Emperor parades on. Wearing as little as is decent, though perhaps he has his sock suspenders and shoes on and a huge bandage on his head, topped with a big bow. His train is "carried" by two attendants, the Empress and Lord Chamberlain walk behind, followed by the Guard Captain and Jack's mother. The entrance is sufficient to halt the cheers and the music and the clapping. Hopefully the audience will find this very funny. The parade comes to a halt. The Emperor positions himself and nods to the Lord Chamberlain

Lord Chamberlain Pray silence for his Highness the Emperor Persimmon.

Emperor Loyal subjects! Most loyal subjects! It's my birthday once again and as you can see I have made an especial effort to appear before you dressed appropriately.

It's more than likely by now that some member of the audience will have shouted out "You've got no clothes on" or similar. However if not, at this point...

Jack enters down the aisle SL *brandishing an axe*

Jack I chopped it down! The Ogre is dead — he fell on his head. Why has the Emperor got no clothes on!?

Encourage the audience to take up the shout. If the audience started earlier, Jack comes in earlier and plays it ad-lib. Jack moves onto the stage. Perhaps he and Abigail can quieten the audience

Emperor What do you mean by that? Let me tell you that this is my birthday suit.

Jack It certainly is.

Emperor This material, peasant, is the most exquisite — magic material — it is invisible to the dimwits of the world, the people with no brains, no sense.

Jack Well, that must be me, cos I can't see it. (*To audience*) Can you?

Uproar

(*To Abigail*) Can you see it, Abigail?

Abigail No! Can you, Father?

Tink Well, er... No, now you mention it!

Abacus And I can't.

Guard Captain I can't either. What about you, Chamberlain?

Lord Chamberlain It's not very clear. I mean — well, no. I can't see it.

Empress Stop that! Stop that all of you. I can see it — it's superb. Persimmon, it makes you look so — so — so ——
Jack Dopey.

All laugh except the Empress and Emperor

Empress *Enough.* We will settle this once and for all. Where are Lord Trust and Lady Promise? Let them be summoned.

Two attendants go off calling for them

They will explain this to you all.

The Attendants return

Attendant 1 There's no sign of them, your Highness.
Attendant 2 They've gone.
Attendant 1 They were last seen driving a coach full of bags, boxes and treasure chests out of the city.
Abacus All our money.
Lord Chamberlain All our gold.
Empress What about my share? Wait for me!

She exits down the aisle SL

Attendant 2 They did leave this envelope for the Emperor.
Emperor Give it to me. And Guard Captain lend me your cloak. This suit is not quite as warm as I hoped it would be.

The envelope and cloak are handed over

(*Taking out a letter and reading it*) It says... "Ever been had?" It was a trick. Wait a minute, there's a P.S. "But never mind. Buy yourself something nice." and there's a million pound note.

Some relief on stage

Tink Let me see it, Sire.

The Emperor hands it to him

It's a forgery.

Act III, Scene 3   63

Emperor What?
Tink (*showing him the note*) Bank of Toyland.
Emperor Does that mean I can only use it when I'm there?
Abacus I'm afraid, Sire. It was part of their trickery.
Tink They tricked me.
Abigail And they tricked me.
Lord Chamberlain They are very clever fellows.
Jack So now they'll be off somewhere tricking other people.

Resignation to this on stage: the harp plays "Hearts and Flowers"

All (*to harp*) That's not funny.

The auditorium door bursts open SL

The Empress pushes in Sly and Wily

Empress Go on. Get along with you before I give you some more bumps and bruises. Go on. Move! Move yourselves. (*She prods them with a stick*)
Emperor They're here. They're back. Now listen, you two, I want a word with you. What about this? (*He opens his cloak like a "flasher"*)
Sly Ow! Don't hit me. I'm bruised all over, your Highness. What can I say, you look splendiforous...
Wily Absolutely magnificentuous, Majesty.
Sly What a suit...
Wily What style...
Sly Only the most handsome, most clever...
Wily ...most intelligent people can see ——
Sly — the wondrous colours, the detailed rich embroidery the ——
Emperor Rubbish!
Wily Pardon.
All (*except Sly and Wily*) Rubbish!
Emperor You tricked me.
Sly }
Wily } (*together*) Oh, no.
All (*except Sly and Wily*) Oh, yes!
Abacus And where's the money?
Tink Yes. Where's the gold?
Lord Chamberlain That you cheated us out of... Where's it all gone?
Jack Wait a minute. Where were these two?
Empress I found them under a large fallen ogre and some sort of plant down near the city wall.

Jack My beanstalk!
Abigail Your ogre!
Jack So the coach with all the money, all the treasure will be there too. We're all rich again.
Emperor (*to Sly and Wily*) You ought to be in prison.
Guard Captain Leave it to me, Sire.

He escorts them off, the two attendants assisting

Empress (*as the two are led off*) Such a clever Emperor, Persimmon. I always knew you were highly intelligent.
Sly (*as he's taken away*) Don't listen to her, Sire. She was in on the trick too.

Sly is dragged off

Emperor What did he mean by that? Were you on their side, my dear?
Empress Oh, no. No. How could you possibly think such a thing? Would I tell you lies? Would I trick you?

All on stage freeze

Tink (*stepping forward*) Oyez.

The harp rings

   Oyez.

The harp rings

   Oyez.

The harp rings

   I like this harp better than the bell. It's got more variety and it seems to know what's happening. It seems to know the truth. I'll explain what I mean. It knew when it was going to be the Emperor's birthday and when anyone tells a lie. It plays.

The harp plays a menacing series of notes or chords

   If it's the truth it plays...

Act III, Scene 3

The harp plays a happy little tune

So when the two tricksters at their trial said —

Sly and Wily are back on SR

Sly
Wily } (*together*) We didn't do it.

The harp plays its menacing sounds

Tink Everyone knew they lied. And when Abi said:
Abigail I didn't forge any money.

The harp plays a happy tune

Tink Everyone knew she told the truth. So the Emperor was able to make the right decisions.
Empress How could you doubt me, Persimmon. I wouldn't ever try to trick or cheat you. I love you so much.

The harp goes to town on the menacing tunes

Tink That really was a whopper. The Emperor had no choice. He had to banish the Empress.
Emperor And never darken my kingdom again.
Empress I shall change my name and go and live with my sisters Cordelia and Regan.

She exits

Lord Chamberlain A wise decision, Sire.

All applaud

Emperor But what will I do for an empress? I need someone to talk to at breakfast, preferably someone who won't interrupt me and tell me what to do. I shall adopt an empress.

Jack's Mother steps forward as the harp plays "My Old Dutch"

Tink So, since Jack's mother became a sort of adopted empress, that made Jack a sort of adopted prince.
Jack Prince Jack.

The harp plays "Some Day My Prince Will Come"

And he had lots of gold, and a hen that laid golden eggs. In fact he'd got almost everything he wanted. (*He turns to Abigail and extends his hand*)

Abigail takes it

The harp plays The Wedding March

The two attendants and the Guard Captain return

All (*except Jack and Abigail*) Aw!
Tink So what I've got to do now is go out and about round the city and proclaim all this good news because I'm the Crier — not a boo-hoo crier — but a sort of yoo-hoo crier. Oh! You know this. This is where you came in.

The harp plays church bells seguing into a Christmas Carol for exeunt

Black-out

THE END

FURNITURE AND PROPERTY LIST

ACT I
Scene 1

Off stage: Papers, large bell, small bell (**Tink**)
Bank notes, weapons (**Sly**)
Proclamation, paper, pen, ledger (**Abacus**)
Rope (**Jack**)
Weapons (**Wily**)
Besom (**Mother**)
Broom (**Mother**)

ACT II
Scene 1

Off stage: Bells (**Tink**)

Scene 2

On stage: Desk. *On it:* papers, ledgers and documents

Off stage: Bills (**Lord Chamberlain**)
Rolling pin (**Mother**)
Knapsack or pockets. *In it:* bags of gold (**Jack**)
Roll of invisible cloth (**Sly**)

ACT III
Scene 1

Strike: Desk

Off stage: Golden egg (**Jack**)
Collecting boxes (**Guard Captain**)

Scene 2

Off stage: Coat hanger (**Sly**)
Collecting box. *In it:* some paltry contents (**Guard Captain**)
Collecting box. *In it:* some paltry contents (**Tink**)
Sack. *In it:* harp (**Jack**)

Scene 3

Set: Flags

Off stage: Bandage (**Abigail**)
Envelope. *In it:* letter (**Attendant 2**)

LIGHTING PLOT

Practical fitting required: nil
Various interior and exterior settings

ACT I

To open: General lighting

No cues

ACT II

To open: General lighting

No cues

ACT III

To open: General lighting

Cue 1	Sound FX: "Fee-fi-fo-fum" *Lights dim*	(Page 59)
Cue 2	Sound FX: chopping increases in volume *Lights dim slowly to Black-out*	(Page 59)
Cue 3	Sound of a falling beanstalk and shouts from the Ogre *Lights back up full*	(Page 59)
Cue 4	Harp plays church bells into Christmas Carol *Black-out*	(Page 66)

EFFECTS PLOT

ACT I

Cue 1	**Wily**: "...you're Sly. I'm Wily." *Mooing off right*	(Page 14)
Cue 2	**Sly**: "It's somewhere in this direction." **Sly** and **Wily** exit *Mooing off right*	(Page 15)
Cue 3	**Abigail**: "Bye, Jack!" *Loud mooing from offstage left*	(Page 16)

ACT II

Cue 4	**Sly**: "Take a seat, Sire!" and catwalk and entrance are set up *Fashion Show music*	(Page 32)

ACT III

Cue 5	**Jack**: "And listen." *Music begins*	(Page 53)
Cue 6	**Jack**: "No! He won't do that, will he?" *Sound FX of the Ogre as stage direction page 54*	(Page 54)
Cue 7	**Jack**: "...down the beanstalk all angry and..." **Mother** nods in agreement *Sound FX of the Ogre as stage direction page 55*	(Page 55)
Cue 8	**Abacus**: "Here we go. One...two..." *Sound FX of the Ogre as stage direction page 59*	(Page 59)
Cue 9	**Tink**: "He'll eat us alive." *Sound FX of the Ogre as stage direction page 59*	(Page 59)

Effects Plot

Cue 10	When ready *Sound FX of chopping*	(Page 59)
Cue 11	Lights dim to Black-out *Sound of falling beanstalk*	(Page 59)
Cue 12	**Tink**: "Let me do the proclaiming." *Carillon rings out*	(Page 60)
Cue 13	**Tink**: "Oyez!" *Another carillon*	(Page 60)
Cue 14	**Tink**: "...three cheers for his Highness — the Emperor!" *Triumphant music*	(Page 60)
Cue 15	**Jack**: "...somewhere tricking other people." *Harp plays "Hearts and Flowers"*	(Page 63)
Cue 16	**Tink**: "Oyez." *Harp rings*	(Page 64)
Cue 17	**Tink**: "Oyez." *Harp rings*	(Page 64)
Cue 18	**Tink**: "Oyez." *Harp rings*	(Page 64)
Cue 19	**Tink**: "...when anyone tells a lie. It plays." *Harp plays a menacing series of notes*	(Page 64)
Cue 20	**Tink**: "If it's the truth it plays..." *Harp plays a happy tune*	(Page 65)
Cue 21	**Sly** and **Wily**: "We didn't do it." *Harp plays menacing sounds*	(Page 65)
Cue 22	**Abigail**: "I didn't forge any money." *Harp plays happy tune*	(Page 65)
Cue 23	**Empress**: "I love you so much." *Harp plays menacing tunes*	(Page 65)

Cue 24	**Emperor**: "I shall adopt an Empress." *Harp plays "My Old Dutch"*	(Page 65)
Cue 25	**Jack**: "Prince Jack." *Harp plays "Some Day My Prince Will Come"*	(Page 66)
Cue 26	**Jack**: "In fact he'd got almost everything he wanted." *Harp plays "The Wedding March"*	(Page 66)
Cue 27	**Tink**: "This is where you came in." *Harp plays church bells into Christmas Carol*	(Page 66)

www.ingramcontent.com/pod-product-compliance
Ingram Content Group UK Ltd.
Pitfield, Milton Keynes, MK11 3LW, UK
UKHW021845210426
5322IPUK00022B/485